One Size Does Not Fit All

One Size Does Not Fit All

Acknowledging and Addressing What's Wrong with American Public Education

Indrek S. Wichman

ROWMAN & LITTLEFIELD
Lanham • Boulder • New York • London

Published by Rowman & Littlefield
A wholly owned subsidiary of The Rowman & Littlefield Publishing Group, Inc.
4501 Forbes Boulevard, Suite 200, Lanham, Maryland 20706
www.rowman.com

Unit A, Whitacre Mews, 26–34 Stannary Street, London SE11 4AB

British Library Cataloguing-in-Publication Information Available

Library of Congress Cataloging-in-Publication Data

ISBN 978-1-4758-3532-8 (hardcover)
ISBN 978-1-4758-3533-5 (paperback)
ISBN 978-1-4758-3534-2 (electronic)

∞™ The paper used in this publication meets the minimum requirements of American National Standard for Information Sciences—Permanence of Paper for Printed Library Materials, ANSI/NISO Z39.48–1992.

Printed in the United States of America

To my wife, Kadri, and the grandparents of our five children: Sven Hjalmar Wichman, Evi (Pari) Wichman, Heiti ("Harry") Roman, and Leelo (Kalm) Roman. The deep questions they raised in their willingness to discuss real and difficult topics was inspiring.

To those who love learning no matter the form it takes.

To those who admire true diversity.

Contents

Contents

Preface

This book is the product of thirty years of admitting, advising, educating, and mentoring students as a professor of mechanical engineering at Michigan State University (MSU).[1] For personal reasons, I was prompted toward reflecting on an important question: *What has the teacher learned from teaching?* What practical, empirical knowledge has been gained by teaching undergraduate and graduate students all these years? What sorts of students will—or will not—learn? How does one's experience inform the practice of education?

One of the curses, and a blessing, of teaching at a large Midwestern school is that the student sample is enormous. MSU is not a tiny, elite private institution such as Bryn Mawr, Smith, Williams, or Swarthmore. One becomes familiar with a great variety of students, and also with a great variety of teaching styles: not everything works for everybody. Unlike the low-enrollment elites, MSU has a vast, intellectually diverse student body.

Even so, at MSU, the distribution of students is not only wide but also deep, with a broad range of student ability. MSU has many outstanding students, whose talents, work ethic, engagement, and performance rival those of students at the elite schools. The MSU Honors College students, in particular, are exceptional. In addition, MSU has several specialized "colleges" such as the James Madison College, the Lyman Briggs College, and the Residential College for the Arts and Humanities, whose academic programs in prelaw and premed attract highly motivated, valedictorian-type students who often go on to attend the Ivies.

These bright youngsters choose to attend MSU possibly for reasons of cost (in-state), geographic proximity and convenience, familiarity, participation as player or fan in big-time athletic programs (football, basketball, hockey), family history and legacy, or social life (friends, fraternities and sororities, the "exciting party environment" of a Big Ten school), and the beautiful, meticulously manicured campus. Teaching these outstanding students has been a pleasure and an honor.

MSU also produces, along with the rest of the BIG (formerly Big Ten), more engineers than any other group of universities in the United States, including the Pacific Coast Twelve universities (PAC-12), the Southeast Conference (SEC) universities, the Ivy League, and all other affiliations. The BIG colleges of engineering and applied science are highly ranked—their lowest ranked program places in the top 10 percent of all American engineering schools.

There is also a serious challenge to teaching students at a large university: the assortment of untalented, unmotivated, disinterested underperformers one encounters in almost every class. These students are responsible for the "camel hump," or bimodal grade distribution, as well as almost all of the difficulties and challenges one experiences in teaching a class.

A standard grade distribution has a few As, more Bs, slightly more Cs, a few Ds, and fewer Fs; the curve goes up toward the middle and down on either side, which is a monomodal or "single-hump" distribution.

By contrast, the bimodal or camel (double) hump distribution shows a second, smaller peak in the Ds, with many more Fs than might be otherwise expected from the single bell. The characteristic camel hump, the result of a recent course I taught, is shown in figure FM.1.

Reflecting on the bimodal grade distribution of a recently taught class, the professor who takes his craft seriously might ask several important, intensely personal questions:

1. Is the poor performance of the students in the second camel hump my fault?
2. Should I teach my course differently or assign a better textbook?
3. Should I cover different material?
4. Did I make the course too hard?
5. Was I uncaring? Insensitive?

There is a way to test these questions:

1. Teach each course differently, even when it is the same course: no rehashing of previous notes and examples.
2. Always change the textbook.
3. Always change each individual lecture as well as lecture content.
4. Always give different exams with new problems.
5. Compare course with sections of the same course taught by other instructors. A direct comparison of class syllabus (material covered) and grades (outcome) shows whether or not one's own courses are easier or harder than anyone else's.

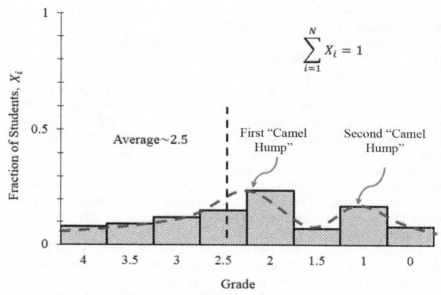

Figure FM.1. *Note:* **Camel hump, or bimodal, grade distribution showing the student fractions x_i receiving grades of 4.0, 3.5, 3.0, 2.5, 2.0, 1.5, 1.0, and 0. These fractions add to unity. $\sum_{i=1}^{N} x_i = 1$, there are two humps, one with a peak near 3.0 and a second much below, in the 1.0 range.**

Using these criteria, a professor will readily ascertain that most of the problems are not self-generated. No matter what text is used, no matter what new and fascinating material is covered, no matter how relevant the course is made through the creative use of examples, no matter how much new technology is introduced, no matter how many problem-solving sessions are scheduled after class and in the evening, the camel hump remains. There is always the second hump of nonperformers. Its baneful and depressing persistence is a topic of conversation among MSU (and other) professors.

Thus, MSU and other large universities in the BIG or elsewhere are excellent laboratories for evaluating American education: We see the best, the worst, and everything in between.

Before diving into how we are educating today's college students, a few more details about my teaching experience may be relevant and illuminating. Over the past quarter-century, I have probably taught more mechanical engineering courses than any of my forty-plus MSU colleagues in mechanical engineering: only one unnamed colleague has a similarly extensive résumé. The number of courses I have currently taught at MSU numbers twenty-one. Many courses I've taught more than ten times, some between five and ten times, others at least three or four times, and only a few once or twice. I have also introduced five new courses at MSU.

Few instructors can claim a more genuinely diverse classroom experience. Many professors teach the same course or two different courses throughout their careers: professors-turned-administrators typically cease teaching altogether. The example of William English "Brit" Kirwan, chancellor in 2014 of the University of Maryland system, is telling. After receiving his PhD, Kirwan taught at Rutgers and other universities until around 1977, when he became department chair of mathematics at Maryland, after which his publications stopped and his classroom teaching likely was greatly diminished, or ceased. Once Kirwan's administrative career began, there was not sufficient time for scholarship or teaching. This is customary and expected. However, it is not widely known off campus that those most responsible for running our universities have the least contact with its core function—classroom education.

Administrators (department chairs, deans, associate deans, or assistants to the associate dean) who do teach will often teach courses having minimal content. So do some full professors, who are jaded and no longer care what their students learn. Lecture time is spent chatting about career choices, social affairs, and football, or telling jokes, folksy stories, and personal anecdotes. I do not teach such "bird" courses. My commitment to what should be happening in the classroom—teaching and learning—has remained steady for more than thirty years.

Acknowledgments

This project, a labor of love, was the product of my free time. I am grateful for the ongoing support, encouragement, perspective, compassion, and humor from my wife and family: from them I have learned that nothing important should be taken too seriously. Without a connection to real living and family, little to none of this book would have materialized.

I also wish to acknowledge my thousands of students at Michigan State University. From all of them, and particularly the extreme top and bottom of the class, I have learned a great deal that is valuable and true about actual learning.

Felicia Chernesky, my copy editor, did a marvelous job of smoothing the tough edges of my writing. I cannot be more thankful for her efforts. The editors at R & L, Dr. Tom Koerner and Ms. Carlie Wall, were a pleasure to work with.

This acknowledgment cannot be complete without mention of the quantitative journalist Mr. Steve Sailer, who knows the meaning of numbers, figures, and statistics, and who excavates fascinating articles on all sorts of subjects: these articles, of course, each lead to many more. Sailer's work led me to the Boe/Shin study, thence to a day-long meeting at the University of Pennsylvania with Dr. Boe himself (thank you, Dr. Boe) and from Penn to other excellent research on quantitative educational statistical analysis.

Finally, I wish to acknowledge, in the abstract, the profound and lasting importance of *facts and evidence*, along with *observation and experience*. Represented in Norse mythology in the figure of Odin, these foundations of our worldly knowledge are ignored, misread, and denied at our peril.

NOTE

1. As a graduate advisor, I admitted graduate students to our program of mechanical engineering.

Introduction

American K–12 public education is based on the notion, founded upon the concepts of egalitarianism in the Declaration of Independence, that *everyone is academically educable*. This notion has led to our current one-size-fits-all system of public education, which always had and continues to yield uneven and often unsatisfactory results. The idea that every person is academically educable has not been subjected to serious scrutiny, nor have its implications been discussed or evaluated in a thoughtful manner.

Instead, discussions of whether everyone is academically educable is true or possible, when they occur, typically degenerate into stakeouts of positions consistent with political ideology. Most debate is reduced to emotionally charged arguments studded with accusations of insensitivity about bigotry, discrimination, poverty, segregation, social injustice, underfunding, "under-resourcing," unequal opportunity, and so forth.

As a result, little progress has been made to address the realities—its weaknesses and failings—except occasionally to tweak the existing system, which is the most expensive in the world and, on average, not impressive. One-size-fits-all education yields a dichotomy, with excellent results for some students (i.e., those who are indeed academically educable) and abysmal results for others (i.e., those who are not academically educable). The qualifier, a subject not addressed in this book, is that even apparently "excellent" students are not being prepared as well as they might be and/or once were.[1]

Evidence for the dichotomy can be seen in how few native-born Americans currently score at the top of the Putnam exams[2] or are represented in the Math Olympiad (an annual middle and high school mathematics competition) or enroll as top students at institutions such as MIT and Cal Tech.

In truth, the reader will agree that we daily see this dichotomy—in the overwhelming numbers of remedial programs, in the college-educated cashiers who cannot make change at the register, in persons who cannot string together two coherent sentences or formulate an argument. There is no compelling need to refer to Cal Tech, Harvard, or the Putnam exams or solely to math and science Olympiads: the evidence is part of our daily lives.

The thesis of this book is that those who fall into the academically underperforming group, which in reality constitutes over 50 percent of America's student population, are underserved by our one-size-fits-all system. For this reason, American public education needs to be reevaluated and retooled.

In the following pages, I discuss American public K–12 education, which is the largest source of students who enter American university engineering, business, science (physics, chemistry, biology), humanities, social science, economics, agriculture, prelaw, premed, and other programs, and with whom their faculty deal on a daily basis. (I do not discuss alternative education systems such as charter or private schools; those systems are worthy of another, separate discussion.)

It is true that all responsible parents would like their children to use their talents for good and virtuous purposes as they grow to become responsible members of society. There is the distinct impression, however, that saying parents would like to have motivated, educated, and productive children who pursue their interests, knacks, and talents is not the same as demonstrating that they are satisfied with the principal features of society today, starting with enforced egalitarianism and ending with a one-size-fits-all system of education that clearly does not serve everyone equally, hence the aforementioned rise of alternatives to public education.

My viewpoint is informed by reality. I focus on facts, not wishful thinking. The evidence from the great half-century American egalitarian experiment is in. What does the evidence say and where does it suggest important and needed reforms can be made? The great ship of America's public education is not sinking, but it is veering off course. And it is easier to right the ship now than in the future. I make the argument here that there is ample room for modest and sensible changes that align with reality and with the realities faced by American public education.

This book is also an attempt to steer between the two extremes of the seemingly endless, perpetually unresolved discussion about education. On the one hand are journalistic and magazine accounts that amount essentially to loosely held-together streams of non sequiturs, unsupported assertions, and anecdotes.[3] On the other hand are dense scholarly treatises with impossible-to-decipher theses whose content is directed through its specialized language and jargon only at similarly trained specialists—a variant of preaching to the choir. This book is meant to provide both opinion and scholarship but takes a common sense approach based on facts, evidence, and above all, experience.

This book is arranged into twelve chapters. The first eight chapters introduce the issues confronting public education and discuss these issues from the standpoint of fact and common knowledge. In chapter 9, the supporting facts for the arguments made in this book, including its thesis, are presented and reviewed in some detail. Chapter 9 also summarizes the independent research of three prominent, highly respected teams of professional education researchers. Finally, chapters 10 to 12 tie together some of the issues raised in chapters 1 through 8 by appealing to the facts outlined and discussed in chapter 9. In this sense, chapter 9 provides the bulk—along with my three-plus decades of academic advising, mentoring, and teaching experience—of support for my thesis that when it comes to public education in America, one size does not fit all.

NOTES

1. The preparation of students for higher learning is discussed extensively in the journal *Academic Questions*, a publication of the National Association of Scholars (www.nas.org), whose mission statement describes it (in part) as "a network of scholars and citizens united by our commitment to academic freedom, disinterested scholarship, and excellence in American higher education." There are, of course, many books on this topic, perhaps none more prescient (and searing) than Richard M. Weaver, *Visions of Order: The Cultural Crisis of Our Time* (Wilmington DE: ISI Press, 2006).

2. The William Lowell Putnam Mathematical Competition, established in 1938, involves a six-hour test to solve twelve problems. In 2010, 4,296 students took the exam with an average score of 11.2 (out of 100) and a median score of 2.

3. This line adapted from Alexander McCall Smith, *At the Villa of Reduced Circumstances* (New York: Anchor, 2005).

Chapter 1

Shortchanging Nonacademic Students

The headlines we consistently encounter, headlines like those listed further in the text—a tiny recent sample of thousands of similar articles over many years—are incorrect and misleading:

- Mathew Lynch, "8 More Reasons the US Education System Is Failing," the *Edvocate*, November 10, 2015, http://www.theedadvocate. org/8-more-reasons-the-us-education-system-is-failing/
- Scott McNealy, "Our Public Education System 'Is Failing,'" *CNBC Commentary*, August 9, 2016, http://www.cnbc.com/2016/08/09/our-public-education-system-is-failing-scott-mcnealy-commentary.html
- Joel Klein, "The Failure of American Schools," *The Atlantic*, June, 2011, https://www.theatlantic.com/magazine/archive/2011/06/the-failure-of-american-schools/3084
- Juan Williams, "The Scandal of K–12 Education: Another School Year Over, Another Lost Opportunity for Millions of Students. Minorities Suffer the Most," *Wall Street Journal*, July 4, 2016, https://www.wsj.com/articles/the-scandal-of-k-12-education-1467673395.

There is no "academic" crisis in American public K–12 education. As will be discussed in these pages, the American crisis in education is in *nonacademic* education.

GOOD ACADEMICS

Academically talented American public school children do extremely well on national and international standardized tests (as will be discussed extensively

1

in chapter 9: "Facts about Education"). When standardized test scores are disaggregated (see chapter 9), they show that the average scores in reading and mathematics of America's white and Asian K–12 students are outstanding, and only slightly lower than the scores of the top achievers, the Koreans, Singaporeans, Finns, Canadians, and Japanese. That is distinguished company for the United States, a large, industrial country that spans five time zones and ten climate zones.

Tiny Singapore and Finland have populations smaller than approximately half the states in America, or about as many people as live in Minnesota. With 130 million residents, Japan has a much larger population than either Singapore or Finland but, being culturally homogeneous, has few of the social complexities that America and its education system must manage.

The overall academic performance of American schoolchildren follows a consistent pattern. Among the largest cohort of students, whites, Americans perform better than white students in European-descended or European countries except for Finland and Canada. Among Hispanics, the next-largest cohort of students, American Hispanics score higher than Hispanics in every majority Latin country of the world.[1] The pattern continues with American blacks, who perform better than black students in other countries. The evidence indicates that we are educating our children about as well as possible: all of our disaggregated subgroups are performing better than similar ethnic or racial subgroups elsewhere.

But there is more to public education than good averaged standardized test scores.

Closer examination shows, like the camel hump or bimodal distribution of figure 1.1, that the American high-scoring cohort is extremely good, whereas the low-scoring cohort is barely mediocre. This camel hump distribution produces the overall so-so, middle-of-the-pack scores that are lambasted by authors of the type cited above.

A method of representing these groups of students as a whole is by using the classic bell curve. Students placing somewhat above the mean can be considered academically educable, while those who land somewhat below the mean cannot generally be considered academically educable past a certain point, or ceiling (figure 1.1). Considering solely average-to-poor students, the lower 50 percent, it becomes obvious that to make comparisons with weak cohorts across the globe does not provide information of much use. And because the bar for the lower cohort of American students is low, scoring better than a mediocre international cohort is, in reality, essentially meaningless progress. In other words, doing better than students in another failing system of education does not help the students in the American system, nor does it provide useful information to educators struggling with the American system and how to improve it.

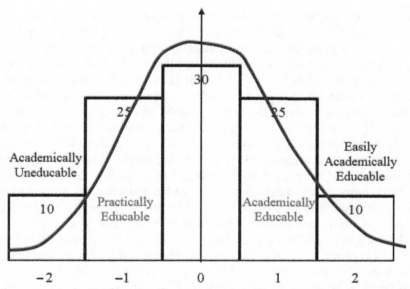

Figure 1.1. *Note:* Graph showing the ability levels of students for academic study in qualitative terms. The numbers 10, 25, 30, 25, and 10 represent very crude percentage of the various student cohorts, and they add to 100. As the right side of the distribution is approached, student academic abilities increase, and vice-versa for the left side. At the very lowest points, the student cohort is academically uneducable and will likely never be able legitimately to complete a K–12 education. Students who fall on the left side of this curve should be encouraged to pursue a trade or vocation—something the current system actively deters.

The takeaway is that America's top academic cohort, consisting mostly (but certainly not exclusively) of its best white and Asian students, is doing well in academic subject matter. The remaining cohorts do well compared with similar cohorts across the globe but on average are very low compared with the top American cohort (chapter 9).

MR. C

Mr. C, a real teacher in Michigan, has been recognized by the parents of his students and his school administration for his stellar teaching, for which he has received several district awards for distinction in teaching. Do teachers like Mr. C, who prepare our top-performing students, deserve a hearty round of applause? The answer is both yes *and* no.

Yes, because teaching excellence is never easily achieved. It requires dedication and engagement to create a classroom climate that breathes life into academic subjects. Students seldom consider math fun or "cool" or easy. Nor is the average student generally enthralled by history, English, or science.

In addition to his regular classroom teaching load, Mr. C teaches "Empires," a once-a-week afterschool storytelling class that all third and fourth graders in the school district may take. He begins class by telling the students stories about the ancient Egyptians, Greeks, and Persians, and then about the Romans, with their conquering armies, martial discipline, and laws. This is followed by several weeks of stories about the vast dominions of the Chinese and the Arabs, and finally an outline of the modern kings and queens of Spain, France, Russia, and England. These conquering empires boasted royal families, nobility, and intrigues of the kind described in Machiavelli's *The Prince* or *One Thousand and One Nights*, which are the true subjects of this marvelous extracurricular history class. Dry-as-dust history is thereby humanized, just as Thucydides humanized his own *History* some 2,500 years ago.

Thus, this is not a scholarly class complete with readings of original sources. Rather, it is meant to be enjoyable and stimulating and to nurture intellectual as well as adventurous pursuits. Mr. C is not doing anything original, but what he does, he does very well. And Mr. C's students—their active young minds ready to soak up the knowledge being offered to them—encounter an engaged and charismatic teacher who instructs and inspires them.

Is this what actually happens?

No. Even singularly dedicated and gifted teachers like Mr. C do not deserve reflexive rounds of applause.

While Mr. C is recognized as an exceptional boots-on-the-ground educator by his school community, his students and their parents love him because he fills a need. The reality is that the community in which Mr. C teaches is eager for the learning environment that Mr. C provides, Mr. C being the embodiment of its fondest wishes for their children's education. Most of his students come from families that strongly support and encourage book learning, and his afterschool class is accordingly packed.

It is not only Mr. C's enthusiasm, dedication, and charisma but also the participation of the parents in this community who have made this extracurricular course possible, by (1) donating snacks and supplies; (2) adjusting their work schedules to pick up their children, since the school buses have already delivered children home at the customary end of the school day; and (3) actively encouraging their children to participate in extracurricular *intellectual* pursuits. Finally, and most important, offering this extracurricular course has been made possible because many of the children enrolled in it are bright and will become the honors students admitted to top universities of the kind mentioned in the preface of this book.

These inquisitive children are supported in their explorations by the excellent values of their families and their community. Mr. C, whom they love and appreciate, reinforces these values by encouraging his students to use their talents.

Had he attempted to offer his extracurricular course in an environment with no parental support and encouragement in a school community uninterested in academic achievement, Mr. C would likely end up lecturing to himself. And any budding talent among his students would have withered on the vine.

TEACHERS AND STUDENT OUTCOMES

One line in the argument about student outcomes can be formulated thus: Good teachers guide their students to achieve to their potential. When the student's ability level is high, the outcome can be exemplary. It is a natural progression for bright and capable students to strive for and achieve excellence in the activities for which they are suited.

It is no surprise that in a community of high-achieving families whose offspring share their natural proclivities (nature) and their intellectually directed interests (nurture), these children perform outstandingly in class. They arrive each morning preloaded for success, only to have it confirmed during the school day. The point is, these children, under the careful and dedicated guidance of their parents, would likely succeed academically under any conditions. The descendants of early-1900s immigrants achieved success not because their parents were privileged, but, first, because they were sired by intelligent parents, and second, because they grew up in a household, in a community, and in a culture that valued striving and intellectual achievement.

One might call this a *virtuous cycle* in contrast with the customary—and much discussed—*vicious cycle*.

Thus, all appears to be fine in our well-to-do community of intellectuals and their academically inclined children. They receive good scores on standardized international tests and, on average, achieve success in public school.

In making this statement, however, we overlook approximately half of the American population whose academic abilities fall below the average (see figure 1.1). This must ever be so, since every average has a mean, and half of the local population cohort, even in an exceptional, supportive community, must lie below that mean: all children of intelligent parents are not as or more intelligent, just as all children of famous models or athletes do not become famous models and athletes.

In addition, the average can shift geographically. The mean of income, for example, may vary so that the 25th percentile in one city or neighborhood is higher than the 75th percentile in another. Why is this? Because there are global averages and local averages. For males being of average height in India, for example (near five feet five inches), is different than being of average height in the Netherlands (six feet): the average height of the world's human beings varies with geographic location.

Nevertheless, in every public school, which is considered a micropopulation, half of the students will be above average in academic ability, and half will be below average in academic ability, regardless of the intelligence of their parents. And the problem is that the American system of public education only focuses on the upper half.

AMERICAN NONACADEMIC EDUCATION—*NOT FINE*, PART 1

Although our public K–12 schools are doing about as well as can reasonably be expected in preparing our academic students for life beyond high school, there is a major problem in the preparation of our nonacademic students for life beyond high school.

Our schools have bad to nonexistent vocational and practical training programs for students who are not interested in pursuing academic subjects or who do not have sufficient ability for purely academic work. As already discussed, based solely on ability, this includes at least 50 percent of America's enrolled high school students, and the numbers will only increase when we include dropouts who have lost interest in academics, whether or not they have academic ability.

There are several options for dealing with this large fraction of our students. This list is not exhaustive:

Option 1: Pretend these students do not exist and continue discussing public education solely as a matter of academics.

Option 2: Acknowledge that these students exist but carry them as long as possible. Then release them into society and pray they find their way.

Option 3: Acknowledge that these students exist and force them to complete an academic course of study regardless of ability, interest, and progress until they graduate and earn a meaningless high school diploma.

The thinking behind *option 1* is typical to highly educated academics and such professionals as lawyers and doctors, who focus only on academics and advocate for "gifted and talented" programs.[2] (I discuss such programs in chapter 4 in the context of helicopter parenting.) For these individuals, the lower cadre of students is irrelevant and invisible.

Option 2, a laissez-faire approach, is typically taken by frustrated but well-meaning middle-class nonintellectuals, who see evidence of student floundering—in the nightly news, in the bumbling clerk at the supermarket checkout line, in the poor report cards of some of their own children—and throw up their hands in futility.

The compromise, *option 3*, is espoused by those who seek a bureaucratic solution that offends as few people as possible, ignores reality, and offers "solutions" that mask the real problems while providing malleable statistics that can be used, if desired, to deceive the community and public-at-large. A combination of options 2 and 3 represents the regnant philosophy in American public schools.

We need not be constrained by these options as our only choices. For the well-being of our students, we should consider an *option 4: Acknowledge that these students exist and do something realistic and constructive to make their K–12 education productive*. It's all the more important that this option be pursued, because the irrefutable empirical evidence shows that this cadre is also the largest group of students.

To start on this path of reform, our K–12 public schools must move beyond the party line, that all students have an equal distribution of academic potential, and that all we need to do to foster and achieve academic excellence is (1) spend more on educational resources, (2) hire excellent and dedicated teachers, and (3) implement progressive policies and programs such as No Child Left Behind and Race to the Top—all of which simply channel more funding at the problems.

The education of a child adds up to *more* than more funding, more resources, more teachers, and more educational initiatives, for it is clear that many schools have done and continue to do more with *less* than their counterparts.

In reality, the education of a child is the drawing out of what is already there. Unfortunately, Americans seem to be uncomfortable admitting that "what is there" is different for every child. Academic underperformance is not an indication of zero intellectual ability, rather it is an indication that many persons are not strong in the theoretical pursuits but may excel in hands-on activities, for example, a musician versus a composer versus a music theorist. Not everyone can be a music theorist.

Reform must begin with the recognition of and acknowledgment that important differences exist in our students' abilities, and that our schools must therefore provide vocational and other forms of practical training for students who have little interest in or aptitude for academic subjects *that is equal to* the training that is provided to students who are academically inclined. Instead of forcing nonacademic children through an "education system" in which they routinely underperform, American K–12 schools should provide alternative forms of education that correspond to their diverse talents and abilities.

AMERICAN NONACADEMIC
EDUCATION—*NOT FINE*, PART 2

Some people are academically talented; others are artistic, compassionate, competitive, courageous, dexterous, vivacious, and so on. It is sometimes the case that one individual possesses many of these traits, but they are far more often heterogeneously distributed throughout the population. The true failure of American public education originates with the official pretense that everyone possesses various traits, good and bad, in equal measure.

Given the reality that academic ability is *not* naturally distributed equally among individuals, what are the alternatives in providing America's students a useful education? Perhaps students should be encouraged to pursue interests that align with their abilities. Note the word *encouraged*, which does not mean required, or forced.

There is a wide spectrum of abilities and many of these are fortunately being discussed openly and frequently, for example, by Mike Rowe, star of the Discovery Channel's *Dirty Jobs*, which showcases strange and at-first-glance repulsive occupations that are in fact extremely challenging and often rewarding. As Rowe takes pains to point out, even relatively ordinary vocations, from electrician to nurse to gardener, will always need workers. Few such professions require the study of abstract and arcane fields of academic knowledge.

A typical example is the young man starting his career as a machinist. He can earn nearly $75 thousand on average, annually, by the time he is in his late twenties, while his high school friend who graduated from college is still tens of thousands in student loan debt. That is quite a head start.

Of course, this discussion is not focused on income but proclivity and interest: To what is each individual school-age child suited? Where should our K–12 students (with guidance) focus their energies? Ideally, responsible American adults should serve as good shepherds for their children. Unfortunately, this often is not the case, and every year motivational speakers visit our high schools to spread this message: "All of the fine students who walk these halls deserve a college education!" (Cue enthusiastic applause.)

As a result, our current American culture (and therefore our public school system) has been based on a bumper-sticker philosophy. *We are all the same! College is for everyone! More is better! Cost is irrelevant! Yes, we can!*

Although such sentiments can be considered noble, we need to stop pretending that what is best for every student is a standard education in history, mathematics, science, literature, and foreign languages. This, as mentioned earlier in the text, is the first step to reforming American K–12 public education.

Peter Wood, president of the National Association of Scholars, has written a thoughtful and elegant summary of the aims of academic education:

1. The pursuit of truth through systematic inquiry.
2. The transmission of cultural and civilizational heritage to a rising generation.
3. The practical preparation of students to work in fields that require advanced study.
4. Insistence on shaping students' minds and character toward an ideal of the educated person.[3]

While it would be difficult to disagree with these goals, what Wood calls the "four horses" of education, it should be clear by now that they lie as far beyond the reach and interest of most people as running the hundred-yard dash in under eleven seconds.

For the average and academically below-average person—half of our population—truth is a matter of living one's daily life honestly; there is no need to read Homer, Virgil, Chaucer, and Shakespeare.

For the academically average or below-average person—half of our population—the transmission of culture and heritage is centered in stable living in a neighborhood or community; there is no need for the counsel of John Jay, James Madison, or Adam Smith.

For half of the population, advanced technical study in physics, chemistry, and mathematics lies beyond our abilities.

Half the population, therefore, will not learn from the training founded on Wood's four horses of education, which benefit, in all reality, only the most academically capable among us, the top 5 to 10 percent (maximum) of Americans. This leaves out the majority of American students whose instructional needs have not been—and continue not to be—addressed.

What half or more of our young students need most, though not exclusively, from a system of public education beyond acculturation and immersion in American history and traditions is technical training, to acquire a valuable skill or trade with which to support oneself and one's family.[4] And yet our schools focus on churning out recruits for ever-more-mediocre colleges and universities where desultory students burn away another four (or five or six or seven) years of their lives pursuing a higher education that is nothing of the kind. For when a good portion of that "learning" consists of remedial courses taught at a third- or fourth-grade level, how can we call it "higher education"? Peter Wood would be the first to agree that remediation has no place in such an institution.

W.E.B. Du Bois wrote, "The final product of our training must be neither a psychologist nor a brickmason, but a man."[5] All well and good, although that man must also function as a self-sufficient, productive citizen of our republic. This will be increasingly difficult with a meaningless high school diploma supplemented by years of remedial college courses.

KEY IDEAS

Despite what we routinely hear broadcast over the news, American academic education, for the academically educable, is in fine shape in the United States, doubtlessly so in the private schools and academies and, for the most part, in the public schools. Chapter 9 fleshes out these details. However, America's nonacademic youth are in poor shape, chained to an unsupportive curriculum unmoored from any postgraduation expectations. It is this cohort of students that is "failing," often quite miserably. Certain minority groups (blacks, Hispanics) generally perform well below the average and thereby reduce America's average test scores to firmly middle-of-the-pack in international comparisons.

It is highly doubtful that the current methods of teaching all of America's youth will ever yield success. An approach rooted in prior experience, tradition, and the results of scientific research (described later in this book) suggests changing the current approach to public education.

NOTES

1. Steve Sailer, "The Amazingly Horrible Test Scores of Students in Puerto Rico," *Unz Review*, July 1, 2015 http://www.unz.com/isteve/the-amazingly-horrible-test-scores-of-students-in-puerto-rico/. As an example, Sailer draws attention to the 2013 National Assessment of Educational Progress (NAEP) exam, which was given in Spanish to Puerto Rican public school students. "Among Puerto Rican 8th graders tested in mathematics in 2013, 95% scored Below Basic, 5% scored Basic, and (to the limits of rounding) 0% scored Proficient, and 0% scored Advanced." By comparison, among American Hispanic students 38 percent scored Below Basic, and among black American students 47 percent scored Below Basic.

2. There are numerous organizations and publications that address the issues and needs of gifted and talented students, including the National Association of Gifted Children (https://www.nagc.org/resources-publications/nagc-publications) and the *Journal for the Education of the Gifted*. The Connecticut State Department of Education has a website devoted to gifted children (http://www.sde.ct.gov/sde/cwp/view.asp?a=2618&q=320940). Many other states have similar websites that direct parents to websites and resources.

3. Peter Wood, "The Sustainability Movement in the American University," *National Association of Scholars*, July 27, 2009, http://www.nas.org/articles/The_Sustainability_Movement_in_the_American_University.

4. As everyone from Socrates onward (and likely before) would say, students, no matter the ability level, require training in things that contribute to virtue and not only in those things that are useful in life. We want honest technicians, plumbers, and lawyers.

5. *W.E.B. Du Bois: A Reader*, ed. David Levering Lewis (1903; Oxford and New York: Oxford University Press, 2007), 61.

Chapter 2

Public Education on Center Stage

The case for public education is usually made by politicians and pundits, including prominent education researchers from institutions such as Harvard and Stanford. Private businesses have attached themselves like carbuncles to public education as its budgets have exploded and, disturbingly, its focus has blurred. Although early twenty-first-century Americans have come to assume that budgets simply get bigger and bigger with time, the recent rate of increase of these budgets has been extraordinary.[1]

In addition to their carrying out their teaching mission, American public schools currently operate as restaurants that serve citizen-healthy breakfasts, lunches, and snacks; as dispensaries of office supplies and materials; as computational facilities with huge computer resources and associated costs; as enormous counseling centers with staffs ready to console and advise the community on topics such as microaggressions; as athletic institutes with state-of-the-art training facilities; and as pension fund guarantors for teachers who "retire" in their late forties and early fifties.

PUBLIC EDUCATION—GOOD FOR DEMOCRACY

Education, a major issue for politicians and policy makers, takes the center stage in every political campaign. The list appearing next provides various quotes in no particular order of historical appearance. These quotes are meant rather to convey an impression of the essence of education as perceived by various thoughtful, witty, and important persons:

- CEO John Dooley of the Virginia Tech Foundation: "The greatest instrument of democracy is education"[2] and "a quality education produces an engaged, enlightened and productive citizenry."[3]

- Benjamin Franklin: "An investment in knowledge pays the best interest."
- George Washington Carver: "Education is the key to unlock the golden door of freedom."
- Edward Everett: "Education is a better safeguard of liberty than a standing army."
- Victor Hugo: "He who opens a school door, closes a prison."
- Bill Gates: "Making sure all our students get a great education, find a career that's fulfilling and rewarding, and have a chance to live out their dreams . . . wouldn't just make us a more successful country—it would also make us a more fair and just one."[4]
- Peter McPherson: "As we celebrate the 150th anniversary of the Morrill Act[5] it is timely to remember the three ideals that drove its creation (in 1862): strengthening democracy by expanding access to higher education to ordinary people, defining the federal government's role in economic development, and improving agricultural production."[6]

These quotes on education make it clear that Americans (and others) throughout the course of our history have seen its benefits, for both individuals and society, and in every sphere of life. The consensus is that educating its citizens is good for a democratic society.

A quarter-century ago, the United States elected its first education president, George H. W. Bush, whose aim, "together with all 50 governors of the United States," was to set goals that "would bring U.S. education to the top of the world rankings by the year 2000."[7] Since that legislation was passed, America's standing has continued to decrease by all global measures of academic assessment.

In 1993, President Bill Clinton "urged passage of Goals 2000: Educate America Act 'so that all Americans can reach internationally competitive standards'."[8] This act became law in 1995 "by a wide, bipartisan congressional majority."[9] Subsequent to passage of this bill, American educational standards and outcomes continued their monotonic decline.

In response, in 2006, President George W. Bush announced his "competitiveness initiative," stating that "the bedrock of America's competitiveness is a well-educated and skilled workforce."[10] Despite the massive expenditures required by the president's "education plan" known as No Child Left Behind, the average education achievement of American students, measured against their counterparts internationally, continued to decline.

President Barack H. Obama instituted his Race to the Top program in 2009, which was closely allied with the Common Core State Standards (CCSS) program, a "state-driven effort to improve K–12 education in America and help children in under-performing school districts."[11] There is much controversy about the CCSS, whose opponents argue that the standards propose educational programs of "dubious academic quality" and moreover represent another intrusion by the federal government into state and local issues.[12]

Despite its importance, and all of the bills and laws passed by Congress, there is little open debate about the basic philosophy of public education. With the advent in the 1960s of President Lyndon B. Johnson's Great Society initiative and programs, John Dewey's progressive education program found full financial and legislative support from the federal government.[13] Fifteen years later, following the creation of the Department of Education (DOE) in 1979 by the Carter administration, the Dewey program became the federally mandated standard practice in American public education. Some might refer to the Deweyan program of education backed by the DOE as training for the aspiring "social justice warrior."

More recently, America's innovative free market system, responding to calls to make public education more inclusive and relevant to social justice, introduced a twist into the education paradigm, namely products marketed and sold to the taxpayer with the benefit of a captive consumer constituency. Public education in the twenty-first century parallels the insurance industry as a publicly mandated program whose profits are privatized: books, materials, miscellaneous supplies, computers, software, educational software, and so forth are all supplied by private companies at tremendous taxpayer expense and great corporate profit.

There are many challenges to educational reform. One is the sheer size of the problem in a country of 330 million, which is why so many people prefer state and local solutions. A second challenge is that since the public education system is ultimately a political matter whose fate is decided by elected officials, it is difficult—if not impossible—to build a meaningful consensus. Politicians will generate disagreements for personal gain whether or not those disagreements have any basis in the evidence. Third, because governmental bureaucracies invariably operate by blurring the notion of accountability, money is no longer an object and costs explode as unionized teachers, staff, and bureaucrats seek to "retire" in their forties and early fifties.[14] There are parallels with higher education in this regard, where costs have also exploded as public legislation and mandates have been passed that "guarantee" government support and subsidies. Fourth, there is the psychological factor: since the Deweyan educational paradigm is essentially unchallenged (charter schools and home schooling being minor factors), nobody wishes to or can cut an education budget. It would be a social stigma and political suicide.

As yet another example of the abuse of American English, diminishing the growth rate of a budget is now called a "spending cut." However, what has typically been reduced is the spending rate: it should be called a "spending rate cut," since the actual budget still increases, though at a *reduced rate*. A good layman's analogy is running uphill: the hill may get less steep as one ascends, but one is still climbing. Going uphill, no matter how gently near the peak (your budget increase), is not the same as going downhill (your budget cut).

The result of using such language when discussing the costs of public education is to shame Americans into silence. What sort of person or board of education wants to cut the education budget—or even reduce its rate of growth—for our wonderful children?

Once the shaming silence has been accomplished, one question remains: *How big will the school budget increase be?* Because:

We need a football field and training equipment, including a state-of-the-art weight room.
It's in.
We need a planetarium.
It's in.[15]
We want a special needs program complete with resident psychologist and aides.
It's in.
We want to provide students free dinner after school in addition to free breakfast before school and free lunch.
It's in.
We need air-conditioned computer rooms staffed and maintained by techies with hardware/software updated annually.
It's in.
We want a board room and posh offices for our well-attired administrators and their numerous noninstructional staff in order to lure top school administrators and personnel.
It's in.

TO QUOTE KURT VONNEGUT: "AND SO IT GOES."[16]

Entrenched lobbies exist at state and national levels to advocate such aggrandizement at public expense. The argument being made here is not that our schools should be Spartan but that huge and rapidly increasing sums are being spent on items whose importance is not obvious for the population at large. Our public schools are among the most expensive and likely the largest and most elaborate in the world,[17] with thriving companies selling textbooks, school supplies, computer equipment, and security system products and services to this ~ 330 million strong public constituency.[18] It is now abundantly clear that the high tech industry will continue to enrich itself as it updates the software and miscellaneous gadgetry associated with and required by the operation of CCSS (or any other federally- or state-mandated education program). All of this adds up to making public education a massive twenty-first century American industry.

And these costly, complex expenditures naturally increase the expectations among parents, the community, and the American public of the quality of education our schools provide. What happens when expectations do not align with reality—and who is responsible?

TEACHER-BASHING, PART 1

Circa 2015 public school students of Detroit were receiving state funding amounting to between $15,000 and $20,000 per pupil each academic year. This was twice the amount public school students were receiving throughout the rest of Michigan.

This extraordinary level of public funding was not producing extraordinary results. The competency rates of Detroit's public school students in mathematics and reading hovered in the single digits. In 2009, Detroit schoolchildren scored *below level* in fourth-grade mathematics at a rate of 69 percent and in eighth-grade mathematics at a rate of 77 percent. Thus,

1. less than one-third of Detroit public school (DPS) students could perform elementary numerical operations.
2. the one-third who scored at level or above were likely only marginally competent.
3. the longer these children attended public school, the worse their test scores became.[19]

Therefore, only about 20 percent of DPS students are *nominally functional* in mathematics in fourth grade and about 13 percent are *nominally functional* in seventh grade, with similarly poor numbers for reading comprehension.[20] The practical implication is that in fifteen to twenty years, two-thirds of Detroit's adults will not be able to understand a bank statement or a simple online article.

These statistics have been exploited to disparage the schools and teachers, who are held directly responsible for the failings of their students. Teachers have been described as falling somewhere between incompetent and criminal, the schools from bad to failed. Articles expressing this viewpoint regularly appear in prestigious magazines and journals.[21] Prominent business executives have called for weeding out (firing) the incompetent teachers who have caused these abysmal results (this will be discussed in "Teacher-Bashing, Part 2").

A nuanced analysis shows that successful public education involves the combined effort of neighborhood, family, and student, and that a crucial basic ingredient in student success is academic inclination and ability.[22] The teacher, along with the school facilities and resources, is a part of the larger picture. This is why Mr. C (see chapter 1) is important to this discussion. He is an excellent teacher in an excellent school. Despite his best efforts, however, Mr. C would likely fail at a "failing school," which operates amid poverty, social decay, and social dysfunction in a climate of ambient lawlessness.

Despite the evidence indicating that these schools are well funded (recall: DPSs operate with budgets that are approximately twice the rest of the state's public schools), the assertion is daily broadcast across the country that our academically worst public schools are insufficiently funded. Consequently, many people still believe that (1) funding is directly proportional to school success, (2) "poor" schools in bad neighborhoods are not well funded, and (3) "poor" schools hire and employ "poor teachers" who are directly responsible for student underperformance. An examination of the belief held by American parents that their children's schools are underfunded (perceptions 1 and 2) can be found in the Heritage Foundation report Does Spending More on Education Improve Academic Achievement?[23]

How does this thinking persist, given the overwhelming empirical evidence to the contrary?

As already mentioned, American public schools are funded at rates unheard of in the rest of the world. We therefore are compelled to ask, given our dedication, our involvement, and our astonishing level of public school funding, why are so many American schools plagued by abysmal performance and other apparently insoluble problems?

For example,

- Why are many American public school graduates unable to add or subtract single-digit numbers or unable to distinguish between multiplication and division?
- Why are teenagers graduated from American high schools when they read at a third-grade level?

There is a connection between these points and the following:

- American students score near the middle-of-the-pack in international tests of reading, mathematics, and science (PISA).
- It has been necessary to make SAT tests progressively simpler since the 1960s.[24]

That the failed products of the K–12 system are then passed along to our colleges and universities has become a familiar story. Consider a 2012 article in the *Chronicle of Higher Education* on "The Education of Dasmine Cathey," who was admitted on a basketball scholarship to the University of Memphis (UM).[25]Although his tuition, room and board, and expenses were fully funded, it quickly became apparent that Cathay functioned academically at a first-grade level, that is, as a six-to-seven-year-old child.

One must ask the hard questions. How can a viable K–12 system produce a student who reads at a first-grade level? How does he "graduate in good standing" with a degree from high school? How is he admitted to an institution calling itself a university?

Dasmine Cathey and the UM is by no means a unique case. In the early-to-mid-2000s, basketball players at the University of North Carolina received high grades for courses requiring no tests and no attendance.[26] In order to move such students along, several university athletic programs have assigned "third persons" to take the student athlete's ACTs and SATs (UM again), and have passed functionally illiterate athletes (Creighton University in Nebraska, Oklahoma State University) and provided fraudulent grading for the purpose of maintaining student academic eligibility (University of Minnesota, University of Georgia).[27]

Many other such mind-boggling offenses by American "universities" have been cataloged,[28] along with proposals for realistic solutions, but it is doubtful, because of the moneyed interests involved, that they will ever be implemented.[29] Intercollegiate athletics is a huge source of income for many universities, even if the monies seldom make it far outside the athletics programs. The arguments in favor of admitting unqualified students are that athletic success drives up the applicant pool and increases the student body, and that also increases donations from alumni. Both of these assertions are dubious. Some recent careful analyses have shown that donors will give to academic programs and libraries regardless of athletic successes, and donors to athletic programs will give regardless of academic success. In unfiltered economistic terms, universities seldom recoup their investments in athletics.[30]

How can Carnegie I Research Universities (schools generally considered to be America's top research universities), of which there are only about 100 in the United States,[31] teach "our banner crop of first-year students" (the universal terminology of college brochures) remedial mathematics (arithmetic, calculation of the slopes of straight lines, etc., which I routinely saw on chalkboards in classrooms in the MSU Engineering Building) and reading comprehension (which I was involved with in a "special" undergraduate course offering)? They should have mastered this material by seventh grade.

According to many education pundits, if all "incompetent" K–12 teachers were replaced with excellent educators, student unpreparedness in college would vanish. And so, the question is, will hiring better teachers fix these problems?

It's doubtful, and here's why.

TEACHER-BASHING, PART 2

Teacher-bashing can be viewed from a different perspective, one that highlights a major disconnect in American education: education policy is determined and directed by those who are not directly involved in education (e.g., politicians, bureaucrats, entertainers, TV/radio pundits, and captains of industry) but eagerly desire to direct it, as seen in the frenetic jockeying for directors of state and federal departments of education during every change in administration. For this reason alone, such people are not qualified for the task.[32]

Consider first various high-profile moguls who have spent hundreds of millions on public K–12 education programs. In most cases, these industrialists present themselves as champions of the average citizen, as people who "passionately" support improving public education. This disconnect is illustrated in Bill Gates, an enthusiastic advocate for high-IQ employees in the high tech industry whose employees represent the narrowest sliver of the top 1 percent of high school graduates who also go on to elite universities. He (more precisely, the Bill & Melinda Gates Foundation) also happens to be the strongest private advocate of CCSS, a program that will yield many millions (possibly much more) to his vast software enterprise.[33] As Wood states, "The Gates Foundation is a private entity, yet it appears to have played a significant role in shaping federal policy and driving significant changes down to the level of state and local jurisdictions across most of the country."[34]

Similarly, companies such as Google give prospective employees tests that quantitatively measure their ability to think far beyond average—and annually eliminates those caught thinking like everyman as part of the undesirable, underperforming 10 percent.[35]

CEOs across the country operate in this manner: privately hiring the best minds while publicly championing the cause of the numerous mediocre and unmotivated. David Welch (now of Silicon Valley's *Vergara*) proposed improving public education by hiring good teachers and firing poor teachers.[36] Bad schools are bad, according to Welch, because of the "bad teachers" they have hired and cannot fire due to union regulations. And while weeding out truly bad teachers and those who have outlived their productivity is a problem that does factor into why our K–12 schools are failing, blaming teachers for student inability to perform is easy but misguided.

So why is it done? For Welch and his foundation, it allows for the distribution of sympathetic press releases and receipt of favorable tax deductions. It also draws media attention away from his less publicly minded business pursuits. Being concerned about America's public schools means David Welch is a good person: the common folk will let him and his money be. A scapegoat like "bad teachers" is necessary because Welch's goal is to divert the media's watchful eye away from his own business practices.[37]

Gates and Welch aren't the only ones to run highly discriminatory operations. Television personalities such as Jon Stewart (retired) and Stephen Colbert have staffs composed of the "best and the brightest"—almost none of whom, by the way, are racial or ethnic minorities or female. The point here, of course, is not that Colbert and Stewart have anything to do with K–12 education but rather they, rather hypocritically, will propose and advocate for fashionable policies and initiatives they would never consider or apply to their own enterprises and pursuits. We must separate what is fashionable from what is true.

And while our politicians, bureaucrats, CEOs, and celebrities, recalling public hangings of local ne'er do wells, offer as a sacrifice the occasional genuinely bad teacher in response to or to ward away public outcry, in reality they care little about the actual education of real students in American public schools. Politicians fashion elaborate unworkable government programs such as No Child Left Behind or Head Start that are bureaucratic and administrative goldmines. Bureaucrats draw high guaranteed salaries, securing employment and bountiful early retirement pensions. CEOs and celebrities live in mansions in gated communities. And all of these people typically send their children to elite boarding schools where they are socialized and educated in the privileged company of other intelligent and motivated young men and women.

Massive, centrally directed programs that are supported by federal, state, and local funds and run according to policy initiatives and prescriptions are, in fact, designed to create mediocrity and dependency. Distantly administered and managed programs are doomed to failure the moment they are funded, in large measure because they do not differentiate among levels of ability but paint with a broad brush over individual character and human difference. In such programs, *everything is for everybody*.

And when the inevitable failures occur—because only 50 percent of American students are academically educable—the teacher takes the blame.

For the educational establishment and lobby, No Child Left Behind and subsequent programs have proven to be a treasure trove that keeps giving. Testing companies thrive, software companies rake in record profits, computers are replaced yearly, and staff and services are added to annual budgets. There is much money changing hands as testing company executives and others reap the material rewards of these programs, at the expense of doing much of any educational good. Recall that test scores are still declining.

Operation Head Start, a program that began during the 1965 War on Poverty, teaches mostly minority children from troubled backgrounds preliminary academic material so that by kindergarten they might compete with their nonminority counterparts. Head Start has since been exposed as having no benefit to participants past age five. Furthermore, the funds spent on Head

Start are uncorrelated with academic results. Its role appears to be little more than a babysitting service for single mothers. The accomplishment correlation is actually inverse, meaning the more money spent on Head Start, the worse the results.

Money circulates in the economy, which is good. But does the money educate our children? And if the elaborate and expensive state and federal programs do not work, is it the fault of the teachers? Is it true that American test scores will rise when all of the "bad teachers" are fired?

ALL ACADEMICS, ALL THE TIME—NO LONGER CREDIBLE

There have been many policy ideas floated about and many policies implemented over the past century, most of them dressed differently but fundamentally the same. The past three decades, for example, have seen the founding of Teach for America, which places recent university graduates as publicly funded "teacher trainees" in mediocre ("bad," "failing") public schools, the enactment of education acts such as President Clinton and Vice President Gore's GOALS2000, President G.W. Bush's No Child Left Behind, and President Obama's Race to the Top (2009), as well as the implementation of the CCSS.

In *The Teacher Wars: A History of America's Most Embattled Profession*, Dana Goldstein (a "writer for publications like *Slate* and *The Atlantic*" and *not*, unsurprisingly, a teacher) asserts that we need to help teachers "do their job in the way that higher achieving nations do: by providing better pre-service instruction, offering newcomers more support from well-trained mentors and opening up the 'black box' classroom so teachers can observe one another without fear and share ideas."[38] Despite Goldstein's noble intentions, this is not a remodeling of our public education system but another small tweak that cannot and will not work.

The Teacher Wars, despite its flawed basic message, states accurately why a fundamental change is necessary in how we "do" public education (the "why" being declining test scores and quantifiable student skills). Until that change occurs, we should remain pessimistic about our educational prospects, as America's youth continues to graduate from our public schools having acquired little real learning and with no demonstrable intellectual or practical skills.

IF WE CHANGE, THERE IS HOPE

In reality, the American system of public education is not progressive. Its once revolutionary (Deweyan) philosophy is more than a century old. Its fundamental flaw is that it does not account for differences in abilities and inclinations but instead seeks to impose a disastrous one-size-fits-all template on students.

Large-scale federal education programs have generally failed. And while the academic upper half of our public school students are doing well—sometimes very well—the lower half is not. These students have been ill-served, and are ill-prepared to live and work in the service economy that has lately been built. A pure service economy requires an academically educated citizenry, an ideal that cannot be realized in America. (No country in the world can field an exclusively service-based economy.)

Only true change will right the ship, not incremental changes such as Goals 2000, No Child Left Behind, Race to the Top, and CCSS, all of which tweak the basic philosophy of the Johnson administration's programs, or advocate for even more of the same, such as college for all high school students. Public education needs an overhaul that can, and will, work for all students when it is tailored to their abilities and inclinations. It is time for a grassroots movement to reclaim a public education mission in the United States based on common sense and facts that addresses the needs of all of America's youth, not only its bookish youth. We cannot keep pretending that everyone can, or should, be academically educated.

KEY IDEAS

Public education for America's youth is certainly a good thing for the Republic, but spending on education has become extravagant and does not seem to be correlated well with results. Of particular concern are large industries that lobby heavily for annual equipment upgrades (in areas that just happen to be their line of business). Many consecutive years of demonstrably mediocre results have led to a particular type of teacher-bashing (fire the bad teachers, run schools like businesses, etc.) by industrialists.

The contention here is that firing bad teachers or running schools like businesses will not improve education. The all-academics-all-the-time model, or the one-size-fits-all model of public education, is guaranteed to yield mediocrity every time, just as is choosing five people from the public for an Olympic swimming relay team. Approximately half of the general population is academically uneducable to anywhere near the degree that current unrealistic expectations are set.

NOTES

1. In Michigan, a new budget for 2016 was negotiated in which an approximately $750 million increase in funding was implemented in order to pay for the deficits

accumulated in previous educational budgets and allegedly to fund future improvements. This is for a system in which approximately 20 percent of its students, *at most*, achieve minimal competency. See "The Facts on Education Funding in Michigan," http://www.michigan.gov/snyder/0,4668,7-277–321385—,00.html for information on Michigan ("number one in the United States for investing in pre-K") and U.S. DOE, 2016 Budget Fact Sheet, https://www2.ed.gov/about/overview/budget/budget16/budget-factsheet.pdf for 2016 information on America at large.

2. Jonathan Witt and Jay W. Richards, "Lord of the Permanent Things: J.R.R. Tolkien's Vision of Liberty and Limited Government," *Intercollegiate Review* (Spring 2015): 20–23, https://home.isi.org/lord-permanent-things-j-r-r-tolkien%E2%80%99s-vision-liberty-and-limited-government. The authors state that "democracy [is a word that Tolkien] wasn't willing even to endorse."

3. John Dooley, "Virginia Tech and the 21st-Century Land-Grant Model," *Virginia Tech Magazine* 35, no. 2 (Winter 2012–2013): 18, http://www.vtmag.vt.edu/winter13/21st-century-land-grant-model.html.

4. Bill Gates, "Teachers Need Real Feedback," TED Talk, transcript highlights, May 2013, at 9:33, https://www.ted.com/talks/bill_gates_teachers_need_real_feedback/transcript?language=en.

5. The 1862 Morrill Act established Land Grant Colleges in the United States for the benefit of those who would study agriculture and engineering with the curricular focus being "scientific agriculture." Michigan Agricultural College, later Michigan State University, "was the nation's pioneer land-grant university and the prototype for the entire land-grant system created when President Lincoln signed the Morrill Act in 1862" (see https://msu.edu/morrill-celebration/history.html).

6. Peter McPherson, "The Land-Grant's Challenge," *Virginia Tech Magazine* 35, no. 2 (Winter 2012–2013): 19, http://www.vtmag.vt.edu/winter13/21st-century-land-grant-model.html.

7. Cited in Eric A. Hanushek, Paul E. Peterson, and Ludger Woessmann, *Achievement Growth: International and U.S. State Trends in Student Performance*, PEPG Report No. 12–03 (Cambridge, MA: Harvard's Program on Education Policy and Governance and Education Next, 2012), 1, https://www.hks.harvard.edu/pepg/PDF/Papers/PEPG12-03_CatchingUp.pdf.

8. Cited in ibid.

9. Ibid.

10. Cited in ibid.

11. Peter W. Wood, ed., *Drilling Through the Core: Why Common Core Is Bad for American Education* (Boston, MA: Pioneer Institute, 2015), 7.

12. Ibid.

13. John Dewey was a famous educational philosopher who advocated for a "materialist" perspective on education, which is justified by being directed toward societal good. One critique among many is provided in Henry T. Edmundson III, *John Dewey and the Decline of American Education* (Wilmington, DE: ISI Books, 2006).

14. It is worth noting that the largest percentage share of any educational budget deals with "future liabilities." See, for example, "The Facts on Education Funding

in Michigan," where Governor Snyder proposes a $750.8 million budget of which $270 million, or 35.9 percent, is directed toward "retirement liabilities to help districts and ensure retirement promises are kept."

15. This is not fictitious. In the Middle Island School District on Long Island (which I attended), the middle school that was built in the 1970s had a planetarium. It was a choice between a planetarium and a pool, and the school board chose the planetarium.

16. Kurt Vonnegut, *Slaughterhouse-Five* (New York: Delacorte, 1969).

17. Julia Ryan, "American Schools vs. the World: Expensive, Unequal, Bad at Math," *Atlantic*, December 3, 2013, https://www.theatlantic.com/education/archive/2013/12/american-schools-vs-the-world-expensive-unequal-bad-at-math/281983/.

18. Trevor Mogg, "Apple Awarded $30M Contract to Supply LA Schools with iPads, Microsoft Not Happy," *Digital Trends*, June 20, 2013, http://www.digitaltrends.com/mobile/apple-awarded-30m-contract-to-supply-la-schools-with-ipads/. This figure is for Los Angeles. The price of such contracts for America's many other large urban centers could become staggering, reaching tens if not hundreds of billions of dollars. The reader may decide whether such expenditures are a wise use of public monies. CCSS, which has a dominant emphasis on technology, will also be a driver for the enrichment of the high-tech industry as it continually develops sophisticated and expensive gadgetry for public (collective) purchase.

19. Detroit Public Schools Community District, "On National Test, 69 Percent of Detroit Children Score Below Basic on Fourth Grade Math; 77 Percent Below Basic on Eighth Grade Math," news release, December 8, 2009, http://detroitk12.org/content/2009/12/08/on-national-test-69-percent-of-detroit-children-score-below-basic-on-fourth-grade-math-77-percent-below-basic-on-eighth-grade-math/.

20. These numbers were obtained as follows: Assuming that 69 percent scored below level, this leaves 31 percent of students, among whom one may assume about one-third or 10 percent of the total did sufficiently well (was functional), while the remaining two-thirds or 20 percent of the total were marginally functional. The same numbers for the 77 percent (10 percent having done well) leaves 13 percent marginally functional at grade level.

21. Jonathan Zimmerman, "Why Is American Teaching So Bad?" *New York Review of Books*, December 4, 2014, http://www.nybooks.com/articles/2014/12/04/why-american-teaching-so-bad/. See also William Johnson, "Confessions of a 'Bad' Teacher," *New York Times Sunday Review*, March 3, 2012, http://www.nytimes.com/2012/03/04/opinion/sunday/confessions-of-a-bad-teacher.html.

22. Robert Weissberg, *Bad Students, Not Bad Schools* (New Brunswick, NJ: Transaction Publishers, 2010).

23. Dan Lips, Shanea J. Watkins, and John Fleming, *Does Spending More on Education Improve Academic Achievement?* no. 2179 (Washington, DC: Heritage Foundation, 2008), available at http://www.heritage.org/education/report/does-spending-more-education-improve-academic-achievement.

24. Peter Wood, "The SAT Upgrade Is a Big Mistake," Minding the Campus, March 9, 2014, http://www.mindingthecampus.com/2014/03/the_sat_upgrade_is_a_big_mista/.

25. Brad Wolverton, "The Education of Dasmine Cathey," *Chronicle of Higher Education*, June 2, 2012, available at http://chronicle.com/article/The-Education-of-Dasmine/132065/.

26. Angela Lumpkin, "Ethical Breaches Disgrace College Football and Basketball," *Phi Kappa Phi Forum* 94, no. 2 (Summer 2014): 29.

27. Ibid.

28. Ibid.

29. Angela Lumpkin, "A Call to Action to Faculty Regarding Intercollegiate Athletics," *Phi Kappa Phi Forum* 88, no. 1 (Winter/Spring 2008): 21–25.

30. Elise Young, "The Gridiron Payoff?" *Inside Higher Ed*, July 3, 2012, https://www.insidehighered.com/news/2012/07/03/report-finds-alumni-giving-among-other-areas-correlated-football-success. Young discusses a study by Michael Anderson, of the University of California at Berkeley. According to Anderson, the positive effects of increased alumni donations, student applications and increased in-state enrollments "would not recoup . . . [the] money a college invested in its athletics program." See also Anderson's more recent research: "The Benefits of College Athletic Success: An Application of the Propensity Score Design" (working paper, University of California, Berkeley, and NBER, January 21, 2016), https://are.berkeley.edu/~mlanderson/pdf/Anderson%20College%20Sports.pdf.

31. According to *Wikipedia*, the 2013 Carnegie Classification of Institutions of Higher Education includes 108 institutions that are classified as "RU/VH: Research Universities (very high research activity)." See also, *The Carnegie Classification of Institutions of Higher Education: 2015 Update Facts & Figures* (Bloomington, IN: Center for Postsecondary Research, Indiana University School of Education, 2015), http://carnegieclassifications.iu.edu/downloads/CCIHE2015-FactsFigures.pdf.

32. J.R.R. Tolkien, in a 1943 letter to his son: "The most improper job of any man, even saints . . . is bossing other men. Not one in a million is fit for it, and least of all those who seek the opportunity." See Bruce Ramsey, "The Implicit Conservatism of 'Lord of the Rings," *Seattle Times*, January 28, 2004, http://old.seattletimes.com/html/opinion/2001845035_rams28.html.

33. Wood, *Drilling Through the Core*, 54–60. See also Lindsey Layton, "How Bill Gates Pulled Off the Swift Common Core Revolution," *Washington Post*, June 4, 2014, https://www.washingtonpost.com/politics/how-bill-gates-pulled-off-the-swift-common-core-revolution/2014/06/07/a830e32e-ec34–11e3–9f5c-9075d5508f0a_story.html?utm_term=.b7066882864c; Susan Berry, "Bill Gates on Common Core Initiative: 'I Believe We Are On The Right Track'," Breitbart.com, October 8, 2015, http://www.breitbart.com/big-government/2015/10/08/bill-gates-common-core-initiative-believe-right-track/; and Alice B. Lloyd, "Gates Foundation Admits Missteps of Common Core," *Weekly Standard*, May 25, 2016, http://www.weeklystandard.com/gates-foundation-admits-missteps-of-common-core/article/2002532.

34. Wood, *Drilling through the Core*, 60.

35. Each year, former General Electric CEO J.F. "Jack" Welch would, according to *Wikipedia*, "fire the bottom 10% of his managers, regardless of absolute performance," https://en.wikipedia.org/wiki/Jack_Welch#cite_note-cohan-15. This practice is referred to in business circles as the "mandatory annual low-performer cut," or

more picturesquely as "rank and yank," which basically means ranking the employees and then yanking the "turkeys" at the lowest end.

36. Harry Sweetland Edwards, "Taking on Teacher Tenure: It's Really Difficult to Fire a Bad Teacher," *Time*, November 3, 2014, 34–39, http://www.texasaft.org/wp-content/uploads/2014/10/Teacher-Tenure-Cover-Story.pdf.

37. Paul Gottfried, "The Left, The State and (Opportunistically as Always) Big Business," *Libertarian Alliance Blog*, January 21, 2015, adapted from Gottfried's address to the 2014 H. L. Mencken Club Conference, at a panel focused on "The Left and the State," https://thelibertarianalliance.com/2015/01/31/the-left-the-state-and-opportunistically-as-always-big-business/.

38. Dana Goldstein, *The Teacher Wars: A History of America's Most Embattled Profession* (New York: Doubleday, 2014). Quotes are taken from Claudia Wallis, "Progress Wars, a review of *The Teacher Wars*," *New York Times*, August 22, 2014, Sunday Book Review, https://www.nytimes.com/2014/08/24/books/review/the-teacher-wars-by-dana-goldstein.html?_r=0.

Chapter 3

The Student and the School

Educating the young has been a topic of concern and debate throughout history: Should it teach to achieve a virtuous citizenry or should it teach practical skills? This question has never been answered.

It has proven critical to the tutelage of such a large and diverse population as we have in the United States that our system of education be founded upon the principles of clarity and honesty. Although one could argue that they are essential to any kind of public policy or endeavor, the lack of clarity and honesty about educational issues has particularly dire consequences for social cohesion; for the safety, prosperity, and happiness of the people; for the common good of posterity (to paraphrase Presidents John Adams and James Madison); and for a thousand other issues large and small. If we can deceive ourselves about the proper education and stewardship of our young, we'll deceive ourselves about everything else.

This and the next five chapters discuss the perceptions, dogmas, and policies that cloud the educational mission and confuses the thinking of everyone connected to this mission, no matter how tangentially. These chapters also examine some of the ways in which these perceptions, dogmas, and policies affect the education of a particular student in a particular school in a particular neighborhood. In other words, I attempt to describe the personal impact of these policy enactments. Just as the declaration of war gets soldiers killed (whose children, exactly?), a policy enactment, especially if it is flawed from the outset, will have unforeseen, unintended, and undesirable consequences. The issues addressed in this chapter are as follows: (1) the central importance of the individual attributes of the student; and (2) the central importance of the stewardship provided by the school that the student attends.

CONFUSION ABOUT THE INDIVIDUAL STUDENT

What causes confusion when the individual student is discussed?

Confusion stems principally from our unwillingness to admit, openly, that not all students possess an above-average ability for academics. We refuse to acknowledge that it is neither "privilege" nor "socioeconomic circumstances" but very often natural aptitude for classroom learning that distinguishes good from mediocre students, just as excellent natural coordination separates good from mediocre athletes, regardless of "social circumstances."

The first step in the miseducation of a student is to pretend that everyone is the same. Note the connection of this misguided notion to confusion.

The crucial first step in the successful education of the student, therefore, is recognizing the student's *actual* interests and abilities.

Two hundred years of scientific research since Rousseau, along with the accompanying accumulation of empirical evidence, has shown that infants are not blank slates.[1] Children arrive at school preloaded, preprogrammed even, for activity. Their talents are distinctive and appear in specific areas, and they show propensities for ways of moving, responding, and understanding.

Children, who possess a persona formed at conception when their double helix is fixed for life, are unique persons. Each child is different from his or her siblings, from his or her peers, neighbors, and fellow citizens. He or she may demonstrate a similar level of talent in a particular activity, for example, achieving a nearly identical time in a distance running event, to another runner, but he is different from the other runner in many ways: different in height, weight, shin-to-calf-length ratio, torso-to-leg-length ratio, lung capacity, blood-pumping capacity, as well as in personality, inclinations, and other psychological attributes and personal interests. Thus, even when the level of excellence in a particular activity is similar, many differences exist between participating individuals. The assertion that two persons are equal, therefore, cannot be aligned with any empirical evidence that the real world offers us. The real world is a banquet of inequality.

In fact, there is no such thing as equality, even though we are taught from an early age to assiduously deploy equal signs. Quantity A is either greater than B or it is less than B: in no case are they ever exactly equal. The foundation of mathematics rests on proofs of inequality. When one writes a particular irrational number (like π) and truncates it using a fixed number of decimal places, inequality and inaccuracy follow.[2] But in mathematics, there are precise ways to quantify inequality. In other words, in mathematics, the question, "How big is the inequality?" can be answered. In social science, this is usually impossible.

How can anyone expect to pinpoint and then measure equality among the complex individual features of humanity? How can anyone expect to locate and then to measure or assess equality among the various groups of humanity separated by geography for hundreds or thousands of years? It has been said that the odds that various geographically separated peoples are identical are smaller than the probability of tossing a coin and landing it on an edge.[3]

It is especially important for a teacher to acknowledge the differences in children and young persons. The basis for a sound education is the presentation to the prospective learner of as many (legal and socially permissible) alternative interests as possible. The astute parent, and teacher, will recognize the talents of said youngster and, one hopes, guide him toward constructive variants of those interests. The youngster can be taught the added benefit of dedication and effort. This means that education, properly understood, is a unique and singular endeavor.

Like a seed, talent must be properly cultivated: If it falls on bad ground it dries up and blows away. There are many people who, as youngsters, displayed prodigious natural talent in some area—only never to have nurtured it. If the person has other interests and abilities one can only wish him luck, though turning one's back on a gift is always a risky thing.

There are many examples of people who developed their one great natural talent. One of them was the late six-foot, five-inch, 275-pound NFL linemen David "Deacon" Jones. Quoted in 2007 as saying, "I had unusual ability, and I knew that. I knew I could play the game, I knew I had the speed, the quickness. I just needed the training," Jones clearly did not believe that every person has the requisite talent to become an NFL lineman.[4] Jones knew he had unusual ability, he developed it, and he is in the Pro Football Hall of Fame.

Unusual ability applies to intellectual as well as athletic pursuits. Talent is primal—then comes opportunity (which does not always come knocking). For this reason, the potentially good student should be exposed to activities that might display and reinforce his talents, and be directed by responsible adults either in the home (which is the best option) or in the wider community, where friends, relatives, school personnel, and so on may recognize the student's talents and abilities. In addition to talent, the young student must be *involved*: interested in exploring this talent, hungry to excel. Only when these four criteria are met and then followed by dedicated practice is success possible. Yet, the greatest condition is talent.

The Norwegian chess prodigy Sven Magnus Carlsen was born in 1990. His father taught Sven and his siblings chess at a young age, and they all became good players. With ordinary effort, Sven became outstanding. In four years, he was a grandmaster. At fourteen, he tied world champion Gary Kasparov. The humiliated ex-world champion stormed out furious and disgusted. In 2013, Carlsen challenged the world champion Viswanathan Anand and is now the reigning champion. He has unusual ability.

The ability to play chess at this level is a distinct mental talent, not something that can be achieved only by numerous hours of practice.

CONFUSION ABOUT THE PUBLIC SCHOOL

There is much confusion about public school education. For example, when we claim that public education underprepares or underserves our students, do we mean that every public school yields the same percentage of excellent students, average students, and mediocre students?

If all schools do not produce the same proportion of good, average, and poor students, then there are differences (nature's inequality again) that must be explained. Why are some schools "good" or "bad"? In what types of neighborhoods do schools "go bad"? What types of students attend "bad" schools?

This isn't a solely a question of physical conditions. Historically, "good" learning can and has taken place in the harshest of conditions. "Bad school," therefore, is another euphemism we must abandon if we wish to advance the discussion (by clearing away confusion). When we speak of a "bad school," what we are really describing is usually a well-appointed building to which a high proportion of *bad students* goes every day. Few scholars and policy makers relish wrestling with the issue of "bad students" since it requires honesty and courage and swimming against a tsunami of political correctness. It is much easier to discuss a difficult subject using clichés and euphemisms: instead of placing responsibility for school failure and underperformance on bad students, it is placed at the foot of inanimate and unresponsive bricks and mortar: "bad schools" indeed.[5]

CONFUSION ABOUT SCHOOL FUNDING

It has been asserted since the creation of the Great Society programs (referred to at the end of chapter 2 as the attempt by the Johnson administration in the 1960s to eliminate social dysfunction, inequality and poverty), that American schools are differentially funded. Is this true?

Case Study from Missouri[6]

In early 2014, Missouri (MO) had 448 public school districts including Normandy, which ranked next to last (meaning 99 percent of MO schools were better) and spent $13,000 per student annually. By contrast, Lindbergh, which ranked 4 out of 448 MO school districts (top 1 percent), spent $7,800 per student annually.

The Lindbergh-Normandy ratio of annual spending per student, $7,800 to $13,000, is equal to 0.6. In other words, Lindbergh operated with slightly more than half the per-pupil funding of Normandy and inverted performance, going from the lowest 1 percent to the top 1 percent in MO school districts.

Furthermore, Normandy is a ten-square-mile district, whereas Lindbergh spans twenty-four square miles. Busing and transportation costs in Lindbergh must be higher than in Normandy, meaning that even fewer funds were available in Lindbergh for the education mission (assuming identical per-mile transportation costs).

The State of Missouri and the federal government (i.e., taxpayers who live outside the district of Normandy) provide 60 percent of Normandy's funding, while Normandy residents provide 40 percent. In Lindbergh, these figures are 8 percent MO plus federal funding, and 92 percent local funding. Thus, the "poor" district is outspending the "rich" district by at least 1.65:1, while performing abysmally and supporting a similarly sized administration and staff, plus clerical, support, advisory, and IT staff—with the largest percentage of its funding coming from communities outside its own district.

Funding disparity is not the problem.

Case Study from New York

In New York City, a community member makes the following assertion about PS 106 in Far Rockaway, Queens: "The 234 kids get no gym or art classes. Instead, they . . . have seen more movies than Siskel and Ebert."[7] The teachers in this school force the students to watch movies during class.

The principal of PS 106, Marcella Sills, is a frequent no-show to her job. Instead, according to community members, Sills has often been spotted after 11:00 a.m., wearing a fur coat and driving a late-model BMW.[8]

In 2015, PS 106 had a $2.6 million school budget. The principal and assistant principal received salaries of $130,000 and $110,000, respectively. The supplies and services budget appeared adequate for the purchase of new books and materials. It is one thing to budget for a proposed purchase, however, and quite another to make the purchase, meaning that there were funds available but they were not being properly spent.

School funding is not the problem at PS 106.

Case Study from Michigan

The Highland Park school system serves the relatively small community of Highland Park, Michigan, which is near Detroit. In 2012, only 22 percent of Highland Park third graders passed the state reading exam and only 10 percent passed the mathematics exam. The word is "passed"—not performed "above level" or "outstandingly." For Highland Park high school students, 10 percent earned a "proficient" in reading, while zero percent scored proficient in mathematics.[9]

In 2007–2008, the Highland Park school system student/staff ratio had been 3,419/358 = 9.55, nearly 10 students for every staff member. By 2011–2012, that ratio had shrunk to 989/153 = 6.46, or about 6.5 students per staff member. According to *Wall Street Journal* reporters Stephanie Banchero and Matthew Dolan, the reason for the academic decline of the school district was the "loss of nearly thirty-percent of its population." In addition, "nearly half of the 11,776 residents live below the poverty line."[10]

Highland Park school system per-pupil spending was $16,500, which was 79.4 percent higher (or higher by a factor of 1.794) than the average $9,200 spent per student across Michigan in 2012. There are many other dysfunctional school districts in Michigan that drove the average up to an already-inflated value ($9,200 in 2012). Returning to Highland Park, this school district "ran up an $11.3 million deficit over its $18.9 million school budget." Banchero and Dolan refer specifically to "poor fiscal stewardship."[11]

A school district spends almost twice as much per pupil as schools throughout the rest of Michigan (including those in "privileged" communities) and yet is in terrible condition.

The school budget is not the problem.

No Disparities in Funding

School funding in many "underprivileged" or "impoverished" public school districts is often on the order of 1.5 to 2 times greater than in "privileged" or "wealthy" communities.

Which leads one to ask how a school is labeled "wealthy" or "privileged" or "advantaged" when it spends much less than what is spent, per pupil, in an "impoverished" or "disadvantaged" school? To be clear, the issue is not *how much* money is being spent, but *how* that money is spent. The data and previous examples indicate that the funds are being poorly managed and spent, possibly criminally, on resources that are not reaching the classroom. And if the resources do reach the classroom, they seem to have no effect or negative effect.

The statistical implication of the preceding discussion, which focused on only three schools but whose general patterns are repeated nationwide, is that test scores and academic performance are negatively correlated with per-pupil public school funding: the lower the funding, the better the performance. Welcome information for school budget planners.

Many carefully researched studies (notes provided in each chapter) have demonstrated that these "poor" schools are often victims of mismanagement by administrators and officials responsible for budgetary expenditures: "To the extent that money is indeed distributed inefficiently within districts (such as Highland Park) it is the result of poor public administration not a lack of appropriate funds."[12] Among the world's wealthiest countries only one or possibly two (Austria, Switzerland) spend more, per student, than the United States.[13]

The facts and raw numbers show that there are no "disparities" in funding: per-pupil funding of minority (black, Latino) students is usually higher than the funding for white and Asian students from "privileged" neighborhoods. Although this reads as if the students from privileged neighborhoods are all white (and Asian) and the students from underprivileged neighborhoods are all black and Latino, this is not strictly true. Indeed, there are very many poor white schools and neighborhoods. What these statistics show, quite clearly and by contrast, is that there is no systemic "racism" against underperforming minorities, a resounding claim in recent years. What they show even more clearly—the takeaway—is that *academic* educational achievement is not tied to funding levels.

According to Jason Richwine in the 2011 Heritage Foundation study, *The Myth of Racial Disparities in Public School Funding*, "These commentators [on disparate funding] are mistaken on two levels. First, increasing school spending has rarely led to better outcomes. Second, and more fundamentally, based on data from the U.S. DOE itself, the assumed funding disparities between racial and ethnic groups *do not exist*" (emphasis in original).[14] Thus, other reasons than alleged "funding disparities" must explain poor performance. Again, malfeasance and mismanagement are likely major factors when "our schools have no money" assertions are made—there will always be little money for the school if it vanishes before reaching the classroom.[15]

Interestingly, many ideas, even threadbare ideas, cannot seem to be eliminated from the public discourse even when a factual tide of evidence contradicts them. Consider briefly a February 2017 article in the *Chronicle of Higher Education* by Brian Rosenberg, president of Macalester College in Minnesota, who asserts that Education Secretary Betsy DeVos "will . . . want to pay particular attention to the challenges facing *underresourced* schools . . . that serve chiefly minority populations" (emphasis added). This, ironically, was one of the "bright ideas" Rosenberg was "passing along" to DeVos.[16] As has been amply discussed, a more appropriate term for these schools might be *overresourced*.

Returning to the subject of scamming in Detroit (and the ways in which resources can disappear), Tresa Baldas, writing in the *Detroit Free Press* in 2016, finds that a "former grants administrator" for the DPSs was charged with "pocketing nearly $1.3 million that was supposed to be used for tutoring services for kids." The accused, Carolyn Starkey-Darden, age 69, the former director of grant development, was "charged by federal prosecutors with billing DPS $1.275 million over seven years for never-delivered tutoring services through companies she created." Starkey-Darden "did this, court records show, by submitting phony documents to the district that included doctored test scores, forged attendance records and parental signatures and fake individual learning plans—all of which went on forms that were required by DPS before payment could be made." Baldas quotes Detroit's FBI chief David Gelios: "Detroit students were cheated twice by this scheme. Students that needed tutoring never received it, and money that could have been spent on other resources was paid to Ms. Starkey-Darden as part of her fraud scheme."[17]

CONFUSION ABOUT SCHOOL RESOURCES

Coupled with the assertion that school funding is too low in many "under-performing" schools is the contention that school resources are inadequate. Like the funding issue, the development, allocation, and use of resources are strongly correlated with their proper or improper management. When there is a lack of accountability, such as when people are hired for expensive tasks they *do not* perform, or when repairs and maintenance *are not done* as scheduled, or when financial resources are diverted to what are termed "more immediate and pressing needs," existing hard resources degrade and the quality of education drops.[18]

Resources decay until they undergo transition from asset to liability.

Often overlooked by administrators with poor vision is that undertaking the daily grind of maintenance and upkeep is far more difficult than constructing a new facility. As winning football coaches say, it is far easier to get to the top than to stay there. It is well for all involved to remember that the administrators at the ribbon-cutting ceremony usually have nothing to do thereafter with the project.

At private educational institutions, a new facility will not be approved for construction until all of the funds for maintenance are available. That is proper planning. What remains, however, is making certain that the services that are budgeted are actually provided: the janitor must sweep and the plumber must plumb, and if they do not perform these tasks it is up to the community to organize cleanup and restoration weekend efforts by the parents to maintain and improve school facilities. Expecting someone else to do one's cleanup is not always a viable option.

PS 109 (Queens, NY)

According to another *New York Post* article examining the case of PS 109 discussed earlier in the text, Marcella Sills was a "no show principal" who "blew buckets of taxpayer dough to redecorate her office and order catered meals, while her students lacked basic supplies and services, including CCSS math and reading books and qualified teachers for special education students."[19] The school nurse's office had no sink, refrigerator, or even a cot. Such items can even be purchased at a secondhand shop.

According to one source, the school library was a mess: "It's a junk room." Another source said that "no substitutes are hired when a teacher is absent—students are divvied up among other classes. A classroom that includes learning-disabled kids doesn't have the required special-ed co-teacher."[20]

When items are cut from the school budget in order to redecorate individual office space and monies are diverted to cover personal extravagances, resources degrade. It is clear from the earlier discussion of this school that the original budgets were adequate.

Highland Park (Detroit, MI)

The Banchero and Dolan *Wall Street Journal* article reports that Highland Park "students and parents complain of dirty classrooms, rationed textbooks, and swimming pools—once used by powerhouse swim teams—that now sit drained of water."[21] Why do schools that are funded at twice the rate of the rest of Michigan have these conditions? What was done with that $7,306 extra funding per pupil ($16,500–$9,200 = $7,300)? For the Highland Park school system, the extra funding comes to about $3.7 million: surely this should serve to pay for reliable contracting services, pool upkeep, and classroom materials as well as a first-rate library!

It is obvious that the additional per-pupil funding was used for other purposes, for various "unbudgeted expenses." Small wonder that the Highland Park school board president said the district's problems—which might easily be labeled "malfeasance," "mismanagement," and "misconduct"—turned into a "runaway train that we could not stop."[22]

Some consider our extravagant spending on public education a reflection of America's benign goodness. Business leaders discuss public education in terms of budgets—as if the topic of education were a financial proposition: fix the budget, fix education. But education is not merely a matter of spending levels and resources nor of "firing bad teachers."

The American taxpayer's money has been streamed into the world's most expensive and elaborate public educational system. But are we getting our money's worth? And who do we blame when American students score in the middle-of-the-pack, somewhere near the Slovakian Republic, on competitive standardized tests?

We're confused. Given the elaborate planning and incredible level of funding, shouldn't American students be placing at the top?

CONFUSION ABOUT TEACHER QUALITY

As discussed in chapter 1, we have found someone to blame: the "bad" teacher. It has been mentioned so often in the media that it has become common knowledge: inadequate learning by our students is caused by bad teaching.

There are several parts of the standard narrative. Bad teachers

- hail from second-rate American teacher education programs that are infected with a "noxious ideology of leftism," where students learn to toe the party line instead of immersing themselves in their discipline and honing their craft.
- do not discipline their students. This approach is a consequence of the "Good Job!" mentality acquired at second-rate education programs.
- and their underperforming, irresponsible, and even criminal behaviors are protected by the teachers unions, to which they pay dues—even to the very moment they shuffle into court in leg irons and orange jumpsuits.

This being said, it is also well known that almost all of our teachers are actually decently prepared. The difference between teachers who are assigned to good schools and those assigned to bad schools is small, maybe even negligible. The key is that good schools have good students, whereas bad schools have bad students. If one transplants teachers at bad schools into good schools, they often metamorphose into excellent, even inspirational teachers. I have witnessed instances of this myself.

It is also true that bad teachers—teachers who are ineffective in the classroom, who teach by rote, who come to class late—exist. There are irresponsible teachers, teachers with drug and alcohol problems, and teachers who sexually abuse their students. Teachers are human beings and similar problems occur at law and investment firms, at mom-and-pop businesses, in automobile repair shops, in symphony orchestras, on sports teams, in editorial offices—even in the Oval Office.

So while we know there are "bad teachers," is it reasonable to assert that poor student performance is the result solely of bad teaching? Although it is convenient to blame teachers, several important variables have been excised from the discussion: student, family, neighborhood, and history.

The issue of chronic underperformance in poor schools carries with it a host of complicated follow-up questions. Is the student intelligent in the scholarly sense? Is the home environment supportive? Is the neighborhood conducive to learning? In each case, one can ask, "Why or why not?" but the answers are not the responsibility of teachers, who function, as Socrates said, only as midwives in the birthing of an educated person.

KEY IDEAS

When addressing the failure of American public education, the nature of the individual student and the school itself must be considered. Students possess diverse abilities and disabilities. Schools can be terribly mismanaged, even when they are funded at twice the level of other public schools in the same states as in the cases described here. Although bad teachers exist, it is generally not the teacher's fault when students underperform. It is also not always the student's fault—though here one touches on the real problem: the one-size-fits-all model of education does not work anywhere.

NOTES

1. Russell D. Hamer, "The Visual World of Infants," *American Scientist* 104, no. 2 (March–April 2016): 96–101, http://www.americanscientist.org/issues/feature/the-visual-world-of-infants. Hamer explains why the assertion by nineteenth-century psychologist William James that the infant's world of sensory perception is a "blooming, buzzing confusion" was erroneous. It is noteworthy that James's assertion, like that of Rousseau, was not based on empirical research or facts, but personal opinion.

2. One can never write the number π exactly. When we write $\pi = 3.14159$ we are accurate to five decimal places, whereas when we write 3.141592 we cut it off at six decimal places. Is the last representation accurate? The seventh digit after the decimal (i.e., after the 2) is 6, so technically we should write 3.141593 for six-digit accuracy. Nevertheless, 3.141593 is *not* equal to 3.1415926535. Even in arithmetic, exact numerical equality is a slippery concept: there will always be round-off error. At what decimal place is one perfectly comfortable using the equal sign?

3. Gregory Cochran and Harry Harpending, *The 10,000 Year Explosion: How Civilization Accelerated Human Evolution* (New York: Basic Books, 2009).

4. Keith Thursby, "David 'Deacon' Jones Dies at 74: Fearsome L.A. Rams Lineman," *Los Angeles Times*, June 3, 2013, http://www.latimes.com/local/obituaries/la-me-0604-deacon-jones-20130604-story.html.

5. Weissberg, *Bad Students*, 33–52.

6. See "Normandy School District," Teacher.org, Teacher Salary and Benefits, http://jobs.teacher.org/school-district/normandy-school-district/.

7. Susan Edelman, "No Books, No Clue at City's Worst School," *New York Post*, January 12, 2014, http://nypost.com/2014/01/12/no-space-no-books-no-leader-no-clue-at-citys-worst-elementary/.

8. Ibid.

9. Stephanie Banchero and Matthew Dolan, "Highland Park Turns over Troubled Operations to For-Profit Charter Firm," *Wall Street Journal*, August 2, 2012, https://www.wsj.com/articles/SB10000872396390443545504577565363559208238.

10. Ibid.

11. Ibid.

12. Jason Richwine, *The Myth of Racial Disparities in Public School Funding* (Washington, DC: The Heritage Foundation, 2011), http://www.heritage.org/education/report/the-myth-racial-disparities-public-school-funding. This report addresses the following accusations: (1) "Children of color in the U. S. continue to be significantly less [funded] than" whites (Linda Darling-Hammond, "Cracks in the Bell Curve: How Education Matters," *Journal of Negro Education* 64, no. 3 [Summer, 1995]: 340–53); (2) "Quality public education for African American and Latino students is persistently threatened as a direct result of inequitable school funding" (NAACP, "Education," http://backup.naacp.org/programs/education/index.htm, April 1, 2011); and (3) "The problem we have is an unfair . . . unequal education system [in America]" ("Schools blamed for Racial Gap in SAT Scores," CNN, August 28, 2001, http://www.cnn.com/2001/fyi/teachers.ednews/08/28/sat.scores/).

13. A reference for the text box, containing excellent informational graphics, is found at USC RossierOnline (https://rossieronline.usc.edu), a website maintained by the University of Southern California Rossier School of Education. Rossier Staff, "U.S. Education Spending and Performance vs. The World [Infographic]," *USC RossierOnline*, February 8, 2011, https://rossieronline.usc.edu/u-s-education-versus-the-world-infographic/.

14. Richwine, *Myth of Racial Disparities*. Richwine's statement implies a *negative* correlation of academic achievement with per-pupil spending, suggesting that the best budgetary policy would be to spend as little as possible on public education.

15. Tresa Baldas, "Feds: New $1.2M Tutoring Scam Uncovered at Detroit Schools," *Detroit Free Press*, May 24, 2016, http://www.freep.com/story/news/local/michigan/detroit/2016/05/23/detroit-public-schools-corruption-tutoring-scam/84787254/.

16. Brian Rosenberg, "My 'Dear Betsy' Letter," Commentary, *Chronicle of Higher Education*, February 17, 2017, http://www.chronicle.com/article/My-Dear-Betsy-Letter/239153.

17. Baldas, "$1.2M Tutoring Scam Uncovered."

18. "Don't Blame Lack of Money for Deplorable Conditions in Detroit Schools: DPS Is a Top-Spending District for Operations and Infrastructure," For the Record, *Michigan Capitol Confidential*, January 22, 2016, http://www.michigancapitolconfidential.com/22092.

19. Susan Edelman and Jeane MacIntosh, "Schools Probe Says to Fire, Ban 'School of No' Principal," *New York Post*, February 18, 2014, http://nypost.com/2014/02/18/education-dept-report-backs-firing-no-show-queens-principal/.

20. Edelman, "No Books, No Clue."

21. Banchero and Dolan, "Highland Park Turns over Troubled Operations."

22. Ibid.

Chapter 4

The Home and the Neighborhood

A large percentage of the students in many American schools live in single-parent households that consist of mother and children, with absentee father(s). According to city records, in the Highland Park, Michigan, neighborhood discussed in chapter 3, there were 1,267 single-parent households and 441 two-parent households, the former outnumbering the latter by a factor of 2.87:1—nearly three to one.[1]

It is the consensus of many serious thinking persons, and even some professional sociologists and social policy analysts, as well as being a cornerstone of practical wisdom through the ages, that the home is the foundation of the school and the community/neighborhood. When the home life is reasonably stable, when parents are involved in a child's activities, and when the ambient environment is safe and secure, student performance is about as good as it gets for that person and that neighborhood, regardless of how academic or nonacademic is the nature of the education.

That is to say, even if the type of education, and its delivery, is ill-suited to many living in that neighborhood (the not-academically educable 50 percent), they will do as well as can be expected of them, performing at or near peak ability.

The opposite is also true. If the neighborhood is unsuited for learning, if the student's parents are largely missing from home and hearth, if the ambient environment is crime-ridden, turbulent, and violent, then regardless of the quality and intensity of instruction, the level of performance will be at or near the minimum of ability. That is to say, even if some of the students are academically educable, fall in the upper 50 percent, they will perform at the low end of that scale.

Too often the discussion centers not on parental involvement, or family and neighborhood stability, but on that now-nebulous concept defined abstractly by economists and politicians called "poverty." As will be discussed, one can purchase used books (e.g., from library sell-offs) for fifty cents or even less, so that a house can be filled with books even if its inhabitants "live in poverty." It is generally not the material but the attitude and the involvement that makes the difference.

THE STUDENT'S HOME LIFE

Princeton lecturer Russell K. Nieli recounts a discussion with a visiting guest speaker, a feminist who lectured on alternative family arrangements.[2] The speaker "explained that the American family had changed very radically over the past few decades" so that alternative families without traditional father and mother were possible, even desirable in our new world order. Vitalized by the nobility of her cause, the speaker requested a show of hands and asked, "How many of you here at Princeton have grown up in a traditional husband-wife family without divorce, stepchildren, or a single parent?"[3]

The outcome of her spontaneous statistical analysis: "To her astonishment and her great disappointment, nearly every student's hand went up."

As Nieli explains it, "The strict admission standards at Princeton and other Ivy Leagues tend to weed out students from troubled family circumstances. There is a good deal of social science research which shows that children from traditional two-parent families raising their own biological children do better on a host of indicators, including academic performance, than children raised under circumstances of divorce, single-parenthood, or stepfamily situations."[4]

Nieli mentions a specific study by a Cornell professor that measured "an extremely low rate of divorce and single parenthood among the parents of Ivy League students."[5] Such students, who "tend to dominate the student body at the more selective colleges and universities such as Princeton . . . do much better in school and on standardized tests than those from other backgrounds, and they usually live in neighborhoods where most of their friends and schoolmates have grown up under similar circumstances."[6]

THE STUDENT'S HOME LIFE: BLACK MALES WHO DO WELL IN COLLEGE

Moving from anecdote to account, and from lofty Princeton to more humble circumstances, consider "From Cellblock to Campus, One Black Man Defies the Data," a 2012 *Chronicle of Higher Education* article by Stacey Patton, who provides a table labeled "A Profile of the Black Men Who Do Well in College."[7] This table features statistical results that, following the pattern of most journalists, Patton does not analyze.

Table 4.1. Academic Success Rates for One- and Two-Parent Black American Males

	Percentage of All Black Families	Successful Black Students (GPA ≥ 3.0)	Success Rate Normed with Percentage of Population
One-parent black families	75	39	39/75 = 0.52
Two-parent black families	25	61	61/25 = 2.44

Note: The first two columns represent percentages of all black families and the percentage of successful students, while the third column normalizes these two numbers to form a ratio. This ratio is evaluated for one- and two-parent black families, showing that the ratio is almost five times bigger for the two-parent families. The success rate among American blacks in producing successful students is five times greater for two-parent families than one-parent families (2.44/0.52 = 4.7).

We focus here on Patton's data for "family structure," which indicate that 61 percent of black male undergraduates who earned a 3.0 average or above (i.e., they were "doing well") had two-parent families (table data do not specify whether these were biological parents or stepparents); 35 percent of the successful students came from single-parent homes; and the remaining 4 percent came from an "other" arrangement.

To proceed, first recall that approximately 25 percent of black families, at most, are two-parent families, because 75 percent of black children are born out of wedlock.[8] Thus, the 61 percent of successful black students come from the two-parent family 25 percent, whereas the 39 percent of successful students come from the one-parent family 75 percent. The quotient 61/25 = 2.44 over 39/75 = 0.52 yields a 4.7:1 rate ratio (table 4.1). Thus, for black American males, two-parent families produce successful students at nearly *five* times the rate of single-parent families. These numbers demonstrate the central importance for educational success of a stable family structure.

Clearly there is more to the story, because some of the students described in Patton's article succeed despite adverse familial circumstances. Important factors *not* included in this table are the student's natural intelligence and drive to achieve. Nevertheless, it would be a grave mistake to disregard the crucial advantages and benefits of a stable family structure to and for a student's education. And while Patton focuses on college students, the key to success reaches back into a student's early childhood, where the influence of family, whether the environment is nurturing or turbulent, is most strongly felt and its impressions most deeply ingrained.

THE HOME: RISE OF THE HELICOPTER PARENT

A latter-day phenomenon, which has arisen as a consequence of the false *everyone-is-academically-educable* narrative, is the proliferation of "gifted and talented" (G&T) programs. Most of the children in these programs are neither gifted nor especially talented, though they usually have above-average (or the top approximately 50 percent) academic ability. What they often have are helicopter parents of the kind discussed in chapter 1, who not unjustifiably wish to separate their child from the slower, academically below-average children.

Thus, G&T programs are often perceived by helicopter parents as a viable means, short of expensive private school, of separating their own educable children from the noneducable students.

Stated differently, the rise of the helicopter parent and the associated G&T programs are among the responses to the seemingly systemic problem that is caused by trying to academically educate everyone. As discussed throughout these pages, many American schools enroll large numbers of students who simply do not belong academically: they have little bookish aptitude or inclination. In addition, some of these students are violent and destructive, and others are being raised in troubled environments that spill over into the classroom.

Amy Chua, author of *Battle Hymn of the Tiger Mother* (Penguin, 2011) makes it clear that helicopter parents are principally motivated by wanting the best for their children in a competitive and unforgiving world. They do not want their children mingling with students who, they correctly understand, will slow them down tremendously. Human intuition often being keen, especially among vigilant parents, they see in a microsecond that students in a class will impede learning. Their G&T child is removed—*pronto*—from that class.

G&T: NOT ALWAYS A GOOD THING

Despite their good intentions, parents need to be honest. Special students are few and rare because they combine two probabilistically uncommon features: (1) high intelligence, and (2) high motivation. People with high-level ability are often not highly motivated. Hard-working individuals of lesser ability will often surpass the gifted. It is also true that gifted people tend to be easily bored. Thus, parents, teachers, and schools should pursue efforts to keep their young, gifted students engaged in order to maintain that motivation and interest.

In an ideal world, the students enrolled in G&T programs should be genuinely special. Instead, these programs often degenerate into classrooms filled with students whose helicopter parents have relentlessly drilled them in a particular, limited skill to avoid their being submerged in a sea of mediocrity comprised of average and below-average students.

The baneful effects of forced G&T are seen in an undergraduate student who came from China to MSU.[9] Jianwei Li observed that her "American classmates . . . had hobbies nurtured from childhood: They did ballet, ran track, sang." Jianwei's helicopter parents forced her to focus exclusively on her academic studies, making her "give up" her interest in traditional Chinese music. There wasn't time for music if she was going to participate in G&T academics.

THE NEIGHBORHOOD

Many homes make a neighborhood, whose "goodness" or "badness" can be deployed to explain almost anything. A "tough" neighborhood is described by some with pride, as a positive factor in personal growth: "I graduated from the school of hard knocks." That same neighborhood becomes a negative when attempts are made to explain delinquent and sociopathic behaviors like gang membership.

In terms of education, we know that the sorts of environments that lead to academic success are the ones described earlier in this text by Russell Nieli. These neighborhoods provide constructive outlets for the exploration of the normal impulses of her youth, largely free of destructive and violent distractions. It is crucial to the neighborhood, to the students, and to education for there to be a critical mass of like-minded neighbors who "buy into" this template.

The benefits of a good neighborhood, of constructive outlets, and the presence of similar neighbors taken together correlate, as Nieli indicates, with higher than average income and academic attainment. The correlation is not perfect, and there are examples of fine and successful children who have troubled backgrounds (see table 4.1) and, conversely, troubled children with good backgrounds. But as the percentage of dysfunctional families and communities rise (i.e., as the neighborhoods decay), troubles metastasize, and mass failure of neighborhood and school follows.

There is a one-to-one correlation between "bad neighborhoods" and "bad schools."[10] Suffice it to say that a "bad neighborhood" will produce an abundance of "bad kids" who will create a very "bad school."[11]

KEY IDEAS

The home and the neighborhood environment are central to success in education, regardless of grade level. Our ignoring or downplaying this fact since the middle 1960s has brought on an educational catastrophe that in many places show no sign of abating. Research, in the form of many sociological studies, as well as intuition, seen in the rise of helicopter parenting and the proliferation of "gifted and talented" programs, amply confirms this. There can be no doubt that two-parent families produce students far more ready for success than single-parent families, and in the case of black males (table 4.1), more ready for success by nearly 500 percent!

And while a stable home and safe neighborhood environment are centrally important to academic success, it is also true that individual talent and ability can trump every negative a particular young person may endure. Thus, we must recognize that natural ability very often yields positive outcomes, regardless of circumstance and condition.

NOTES

1. See "Highland Park, Michigan," City-Data.com, http://www.city-data.com/city/Highland-Park-Michigan.html.

2. Russell K. Nieli, "Preach What You Practice: Charles Murray on Our New Class Divide," *Academic Questions* 25, no. 2 (Summer 2012): 286–96.

3. Ibid., 286.

4. Ibid.

5. Ibid., 287.

6. Ibid.

7. Stacey Patton, "From Cellblock to Campus, One Black Man Defies the Data," *Chronicle of Higher Education*, November 2, 2012, B9—B13, http://www.chronicle.com/article/from-cellblock-to-campus-one/135294.

8. Walter E. Williams, "The True Black Tragedy: Illegitimacy Rate of Nearly 75%," cnsnews.com, May 19, 2015, http://www.cnsnews.com/commentary/walter-e-williams/true-black-tragedy-illegitimacy-rate-nearly-75.

9. Karin Fischler, "A Year Inside the Journey from China to East Lansing," *Chronicle of Higher Education*, September 6, 2013, A42.

10. Weissberg, *Bad Students*.

11. Ibid., chap. 2, 23–52, contains an extensive discussion of this fact.

Chapter 5

A Muddled Mission

Mission confusion is, at its core, philosophical confusion. If the ideas about education are muddled, what hope does the educational mission have for success? We see with hindsight that the philosophy of American secondary school education for the past 100 years is muddled. A key part of that confusion is the one-size-fits-all mentality that has slowly evolved into its current counterproductive state. The American K–12 education system aspires to an unattainable ideal—academic education for everyone—which this book asserts is futile.

This short chapter discusses reigning confusion in our educational objectives and expectations. Some of the most egregious statements are made by those who know better but are clearly doing so for political effect. But while today's politicians and public servants living in gated communities can afford expensive, elite private schools for their children, the average middle-class family cannot, and the consequences for such families are, unfortunately, less than desirable.

MUDDLED OBJECTIVES

Every American president since Lyndon B. Johnson has defined a substantial part of his domestic agenda in terms of a federal education program.[1] The U.S. DOE was established in 1979 under President Jimmy Carter (1976–1980). Even though federal dollars represent only about 10 percent of a given school's budget, plus or minus a few percent, it is *real leverage*, which is why every public school complies with federal program dictates. Thus, the DOE exerts control far beyond its proportion in the school budget because that one-tenth funding increment makes the difference between an inadequate and an adequate budget.

Here is a list of many failed but ever more generously funded federal education programs, or missions.

In his 1990 State of the Union address, President George H. W. Bush inaugurated the America 2000 program that discussed and formulated curriculum standards but ultimately did not meet its heady predictions of vaulting America's high school students into the top tier. By 2010, over twenty years after this program was implemented, the United States did not climb the ranks in international education rankings. Instead, public school quality continuously declined as the average performance of American school children on standardized tests spiraled downward. The same is true of Bill Clinton's subsequent (1994) education initiative, GOALS 2000, during which average public school quality and test scores continued their decline.

In the coming years, in addition to domestic woes (decaying infrastructure, greatly reduced basic R&D, industrial disinvestment, unemployment), tens of millions of immigrants entered the United States, placing additional burdens on American neighborhoods and schools. George W. Bush's response, the No Child Left Behind program (2001), failed in weak schools that needed better direction and guidance and also produced few measurable improvements even in strong schools.

Continuing this thirty-year trend, Barack Obama's Race to the Top (2009) also failed to meet its objectives. Another program, the CCSS, which had its roots in No Child Left Behind, was announced in 2009 and quickly and extensively implemented in 2010—and almost immediately widely debated and criticized.[2]

Advocates of CCSS mention (and laud) its decentralization, that it was developed by local academics interested in academic progress and improvement, and that it focuses on the improved preparation of students for the challenges of the twenty-first century. Colleges and universities currently "spend $7 billion a year on remedial courses for their students, while the students spend an estimated $3 billion or more annually to take those courses."[3] Thus, "higher education has invested billions of public dollars every year in so-called remedial education to prepare students for basic mathematics and writing."[4]

The chancellors of the University of Maryland, the California State System, and the State University (System) of New York have creatively called this gap in American K–12 education the "preparation gap," and have assured Americans that the "Common Core standards . . . will help close the preparation gap and set students on the path to prosperity."[5] We have heard this siren song before.

"UNIVERSAL" ACADEMIC EDUCATION

The common flaw in all of these programs and policies originates with a muddled philosophy of the goals of education: its mission. The academic public education of our youth is something contemporary Americans have been seduced into believing should be "universal" (since "college" is the *de facto* end game). And for this reason, we have painted ourselves into the proverbial corner by worshipping at the altar of infinite progress and universal social uplift.

An idealized goal such as "Universal Academic Education" is possible only if we redefine its meaning and content. Indeed, every human being is educable in some way. That way, however, must be clarified using sharper tools than those deployed by ambitious bureaucrats and politicians. In opposition to this biological and social reality, the current meaning of Universal Academic Education has foolishly been defined upward, until Americans accept the notion that every child is academically educable, even into college—once again mistakenly trying to make a one-size-fits-all system of public education fit.

Some may recall Garrison Keillor's absurdist characterization in his *Prairie Home Companion* skits of the fictitious town of Lake Woebegone, where "all the women are strong, all the men are good-looking, and all the children are above average." The goal of No Child Left Behind actually was to raise every student to an above-average level of academic accomplishment! This would be achieved by a system of high standards that eliminated soft expectations, which held everybody back, particularly our underperforming minorities. The entire program, and every one before it, was disconnected from reality.

MUDDLED EXPECTATIONS

The bar in the muddled American public education system has been set impossibly high. America's one-size-fits-all model asserts that all children are ready for academic grooming and, once their K–12 preparation is complete, all will be able to continue their scholarly pursuits at a college or university. The goal in our new Universal Finance-Based Economy is a white-collar job for everyone.

President Clinton said it loud and clear, President Bush supported it implicitly, and President Obama reiterated it explicitly: *Everyone deserves to attend college.*

Unfortunately, reality must be respected. More than half of America's young people are not academically educable—up to and through what has traditionally been called the twelfth grade.

This type of honesty, however, is discouraged, and stating that someone is academically incapable is considered a grave insult. As a result, euphemisms are used to describe children who cannot or will not learn: developmentally challenged, academically unresponsive, and differently class-groomed.

Although this is a sensitive subject, and a measure of politeness should be the norm, the truth must be uttered without restraint or apology. Not everyone is academically educable and for this reason, a one-size-fits-all system is a terrible proposition. In addition to not serving the needs of youngsters who simply cannot learn the academic subjects, this program ill serves those who can but are not interested in pure academics. These students, often talented, are motivated by hands-on learning, which they must either defer to the time their compulsory academics are finished (grade twelve) or which they can pursue at the cost of doing poorly in their academic subjects. Neither choice is optimal.

The issue is being discussed, though fitfully and sporadically, the most public being Mike Rowe of the hit TV show *Dirty Jobs*. Articles are being written about youngsters for whom the specialty school or program is the first step toward success.[6] We simply cannot continue to pretend that everyone is academically educable, even when they carry no other obvious baggage.

KEY IDEAS

It is one thing for everyone to be assured of an equal opportunity. There can be no assurance of an equal outcome. We all once competed in an elementary school 100-yard dash and one of our schoolmates was always the fastest. As simple as this story is, it is the obvious argument against the equal-outcome school of muddled social philosophy. We are not equally fast, and a one-size-fits-all program is a disservice to everyone who cannot compete much less win the race. A better means, rooted in unequal reality while also gainfully supporting the healthy diversity of American society, must be found to educate our students to their abilities.

Rumblings to this effect are slowly becoming audible.

NOTES

1. Valeri Strauss, "Who Was the 'Best' Education President?" *Washington Post*, November 21, 2011, https://www.washingtonpost.com/blogs/answer-sheet/post/who-was-the-best-education-president/2011/11/20/gIQAL3kggN_blog.html?utm_term=

.8fc00c380d79. Citing Kenneth Wong, education chair at Brown University and director of Brown's Urban Education Policy Program:

> Title I of the Elementary and Secondary Education Act of 1965 . . . launched the system of federal grants-in-aid in low-income schools [and was] a central part of the president's War on Poverty. Johnson's vision was to address poverty with greater access to schooling opportunities, thereby enabling all students to become participants in the work force and full citizens in our democracy. The 1965 ESEA continues to shape its contemporary configurations, including Improving America's Schools Act in 1983 and the No Child Left Behind Act of 2001.

2. Wood, *Drilling Through the Core*, chaps. 5–7.

3. William E. (Brit) Kirwan, Timothy P. White, and Nancy Zimpher, "Use the Common Core. Use It Widely, Use It Well," *Chronicle of Higher Education*, June 20, 2014, A64, http://www.chronicle.com/article/Use-the-Common-Core-Use-It/147007.

4. Ibid.

5. Ibid.

6. Nicholas Wyman, "Why We Desperately Need to Bring Back Vocational Training in Schools," *Forbes*, September 1, 2015, https://www.forbes.com/sites/nicholaswyman/2015/09/01/why-we-desperately-need-to-bring-back-vocational-training-in-schools/2/#7a56bc3b56f8.

Chapter 6

Sociological and Political Confusion

Largely driven by the DOE post-1980, an official narrative of public education has taken root that attempts to reject other narratives. That narrative is principally Deweyan, or "progressive," and its authors have deployed an ideology of guilt to control public discourse on the issue of education. In this narrative, an assortment of North European-descended peoples created a discriminatory public education system that purposefully disenfranchised everyone else. The disenfranchised class was subjugated and oppressed, and the oppression continues unabated to this day.

In this malignant official narrative, education is discussed in terms of class conflict and opposition. Erased from the discussion is the role played by human proclivities, interests, and aspirations. As a consequence, in present-day America, the language of measured discourse has been permanently distorted: there is a default plaintiff, which is the oppressed or subjugated class, and a default defendant, which is the advantaged class.

Thus, a guilt complex has grown and metastasized and has—among a sizeable fraction of the former oppressing class of North European–descended people—birthed a "we owe you" mentality that stands at the core of America's muddled educational mission. This "we owe you" mentality has engendered the futile attempt to set things right by asserting, falsely, that everyone is indeed academically educable, and all that we (i.e., well-meaning or "good" persons) need to do is to make sure that education is delivered. The road to perdition is paved with what appears to be, at the outset, good intentions.

This chapter briefly discusses various confused statements and writings about topics of sociology and social programs and arrangements that have yielded much mischief in public education.

CRIME

Everyone knows that in all of America's inner city ghettos (Atlanta, Detroit, Houston, Los Angeles, Memphis, New York, Philadelphia, St. Louis, Washington, DC), the public schools are struggling and the numbers confirm it. All of these places have very high crime rates, some ten times the national average, and far higher than average illegitimacy rates. Given such systemic failure, it is reasonable to believe that crime, illegitimacy, and school performance are correlated.

The trouble with arguing these points with sociologists and politicians is that social problems do not yield to clean mathematical proofs. The statement, "You cannot prove that," though true, has ever been the sophist's fallback position. Why is that? Because there can never be definitive proof that crime and illegitimacy are *causal* for low test scores and high dropout rates. And apparently if you cannot prove your point the sophistic sociologist wins the argument.

Instead of winning arguments using dubious tactics, sociologists should recall that sociology seeks only to quantify—to the extent that it is possible—human social behavior. She requires the use of quantitative methods to describe the evidence in cooperation with reason, wisdom, and experience as regulated by the principles of honesty and objectivity.

Given the aforementioned empirical results about American inner cities, it is a challenge indeed to demonstrate that ambient crime, social dysfunction, illegitimacy, and chaos do not act in concert like the four horsemen of the apocalypse to the detriment of public education. Many sociologists and public policy types twist themselves into knots trying to do so. Nevertheless, and as stated previously by Russell Nieli (chapter 4), there is a wealth of statistical, factual, and anecdotal material that describes the detrimental effect of crime, social dysfunction, illegitimacy, and chaos on individual education and on broader social outcomes.

In a 2016 television interview, several school teachers discussed the consequences of criminal behavior in American schools, whether by actual students or local residents, leaving no doubt that it has a stunningly negative effect.[1] If confusion about the crime rate—its origins, and presence in some neighborhoods—can be cleared up, progress can then be made toward improving K–12 public education in areas that most need it.

A first step is to acknowledge that a problem exists. The second step is to address that problem by admitting that it has a huge deleterious effect on the students in that school (and in that neighborhood). Removing the bad apples is crucial to any hope and possibility of rehabilitation.[2]

SOCIAL JUSTICE

The desire for social justice was built into the American constitution, as well as the founding documents of countries such as Iceland, the world's oldest parliamentary democracy. The Romans wrote about social justice, as did even older civilizations. Who has ever wished to live in a cruel, oppressive family, neighborhood, community, state, or country?

"Social justice," however, has lately been reconfigured in the public imagination by a bogus metric called *equality*. In its current definition, true justice is achieved once inequality or the absence of equality has been eradicated. The doctrine has a beguiling, childlike simplicity, but it has at least two serious flaws: (1) nobody has described how equality or degrees of inequality can be measured; and (2) even if there were agreement on how to measure equality, in practice equality is impossible to attain. Thus, failure is guaranteed and the "social justice warrior's" struggle must continue forever.

THE GAP

Particularly, vexing to educationists, bureaucrats, politicians, and, by extension, the voting public, has been, and continues to be, the poor performance of various, *though by no means all*, minority populations. This is called the "gap" in educational achievement. Note the word "achievement" and not "opportunity."

Great sociological, political, and policy confusion arose in asking a combustible, indeed explosive, question: Why are test scores and test results not equal among the various segments of the American population? Asking this question gave birth to a spectrum of malicious allegations—bigotry, discrimination, prejudice, classism, racism, sexism, etc.

A very good case can be made that closing achievement gaps has been the principal objective of the American public education establishment.[3] And the chaos and confusion caused by this "close the gap" approach has been detrimental to potentially good students who are swept up in every faddish experiment performed on America's public school population, adding a layer of meddling in educational programming and operations that many have argued has yielded no benefits.[4]

Rhetoric about the gap has generally been incendiary and accusatory, not measured and constructive. Finger-pointing terminology is deployed, its goal being to generate confrontation, controversy, and confusion, and not to foster agreement and resolution. Explanations for the gap include (1) insufficient funding of minority (racial) versus majority schools, (2) low minority student self-esteem, (3) individual and institutional discrimination, (4) lack of minority teachers and mentors, (5) poor or "underresourced" school facilities, (6) poverty, and (7) lead poisoning.

SOCIAL MISCHARACTERIZATION

A great deal of trouble and conflict that spills over into public education also arises because of common, insidious social mischaracterization. Regarding explanations for the gap, for example, only inferred discrimination can be quantified, and then only if one agrees with the premises. For the as-yet unquantified explanations—discrimination, racism, structural racism, and differential mentoring (i.e., preferential mentoring of some groups of students over others)—causality can be asserted but proof is impossible. The best that can be done, perhaps, is to develop quantitative methods of explanation such as "path theory," which employs a mathematical and abstract means for sorting out causes from effects.[5]

Social mischaracterization elevates emotional content at the expense of facts. The potency of sentimental arguments is measured by the sympathy they produce. Sometimes this takes the form of riots, at other times it materializes as anonymous Internet insults. In polite society, it manifests as required "sensitivity training" and group shaming. Fact-free theories furnish those who believe them with the unshakable conviction characteristic of the uninformed.

The impossibility of verification (or falsification) is the bogus theory's greatest source of power. This is also true for theories of "bigotry," "discrimination," "structural and institutional racism," and similar premises underlying government educational programs that justify their missions by using accusations that cannot be verified.

There is also a more nefarious consequence of applying unverifiable social theories: they claim the existence of an underperforming and disadvantaged victim (the out-group), who is exploited and discriminated against by a monolithic advantaged population or institution (the in-group). Therefore, everything that is wrong in the "victim's" life, no matter how minor, is caused by an exploitative, oppressive other.

A layman's version of the Great American Victimhood Narrative is articulated in Bob Dylan's "Positively 4th Street" lyrics, which begins, "You got a lotta nerve/ To say you are my friend/When I was down/you just stood there grinning," and continues:

> You see me on the street
> You always act surprised
> You say, "How are you?" "Good luck"

But you don't mean it
When you know as well as me
You'd rather see me paralyzed
Why don't you just come out once
And scream it?[6]

One might ask Dylan, does anyone know someone who has wished another person was paralyzed? And more important, who precisely are you accusing?

Unverifiable theories and Dylanesque pop songs make broad accusations of racism, bigotry, structural prejudice, and so on by setting up straw men and bludgeoning them until they are paralyzed. But society is composed of flesh-and-blood persons. And flesh-and-blood people do not typically wish to see any other flesh-and-blood people paralyzed. Most of us probably embrace, whether consciously or not, the golden rule of doing unto others as we'd have done unto ourselves.

INFERRED DISCRIMINATION

Inferred discrimination can allegedly be quantified in the following example. Blacks make up 13 percent of the American population, but just 1 percent of America's engineers. The progressive sociologist or journalist then asserts that the 12 percent disparity represents racial discrimination in engineering. To compensate for past discrimination, minorities are over-recruited into engineering via affirmative action initiatives and programs (which include simplified curricula and lowered standards). A common justification for such reverse discrimination is that these programs bring highly valued "different perspectives" to engineering.

Inferred discrimination theory postulates that the extent to which a group of persons has been discriminated against is a function of the difference between its percentage in the population (13, for the above-mentioned example) and the percentage represented in a particular field (1, for the earlier mentioned example), the difference being 12: 13–1 = 12 for blacks in engineering.

Here is another example. Females constitute over 50 percent of the adult population but only 10 percent of the nation's engineers, which, for the progressive, is a factor of 5 underrepresentation, an improvement over the factor of 13 for black engineers. The inference is that there is active discrimination involved in this disproportionate outcome as well. (There appears to be a great deal of discrimination taking place.)

The problem with this thinking (and the progressive's assertions) was pointed out decades ago: "There is no simple relationship between a group's upward social mobility and the amount of discrimination it suffered in the past. Discrimination can cause low rates of upward mobility, but it does not automatically lead to poor achievement."[7] Thus, Japanese and Chinese Americans have suffered discrimination but have generally done well, particularly in the professions.

An example of the sociologist's inferred discrimination would be the comparatively smaller numbers of females on many college campuses in the 1960s. According to the theory, this result was "caused" by discrimination by males against females in their quest to be admitted to college. Now, some fifty years later, the tables have turned and many universities, like MSU, are nearly 60 percent female, and rising. Can we infer that American women are "discriminating" against American men in college admissions? How did American women, "meek" and "discriminated against," transform themselves into aggressive and oppressive discriminators in fifty short years? There must be more to this story than oscillating discrimination and remediation.

The confusion caused by willful social mischaracterization, such as inferred discrimination, must be stopped. Sociologists who engage in this form of dishonesty must be called out and their work challenged.

KEY IDEAS

We look to scholars, public intellectuals, and pundits for direction and guidance on issues of national concern such as public education. It does no good to misrepresent and minimize (or excuse) destructive behaviors such as fatherlessness and crime, particularly in struggling neighborhoods. And it does the polity no good to have to address the civic unrest caused by social mischaracterization, the use of pejoratives and loaded language designed, in reality, not to solve problems but to exacerbate tensions among America's various racial and ethnic populations. Why are some individuals and organizations interested in fanning the flames? Probably because they profit from the state of chaos and the "fixes" such unrest engenders.

NOTES

1. This report appeared in the Jesse "Watters' World" segment on the April 11, 2016, *O'Reilly Factor*. The report consists of four interviews with active and retired teachers, all of them minorities. The retired teacher, who stopped teaching over concerns for her safety, always kept her desk close to the classroom door so she had a viable means of escape when the class became violent. All of the teachers were disturbed by the levels of violence and crime in their schools.

2. Weissberg, *Bad Students*, chap. 3.

3. See Raymond Wolters, *The Long Crusade: Profiles in Education Reform, 1967–2014* (Whitefish, MT: Washington Summit Publishers, 2015) and "Why Education Reform Failed," *National Policy Institute*, August 28, 2015, http://www. npiamerica.org/research/why-school-reform-failed. See also Richard D. Kahlenberg, "Learning from James Coleman," *National Affairs*, issue 144 (Summer 2001): 54–72, http://www.nationalaffairs.com/public_interest/detail/learning-from-james-coleman. An extremely thorough argument on this topic is found in Weissberg, *Bad Students*, 83–113.

4. Weissberg, *Bad Students*, 83–113.

5. D.C. Rao, N.E. Morton, R.C. Elston, and S. Yee, "Causal Analysis of Academic Performance," *Behavior Genetics* 7, no. 2 (March 1977): 147–59. In this work, the authors examine the relationship between causes and effects using mathematical methods of analysis. Their article shows that "American schools do not significantly modify socioeconomic differences in academic performance and that little of the observed racial differences in academic performance is causal." Thus, "for two races differing by 15 IQ points, the differential if social class were randomized would only be about 3 points."

6. Bob Dylan, "Positively 4th Street," *Columbia Records*, September 7, 1965; official lyrics available at https://bobdylan.com/songs/positively-4th-street/.

7. William R. Beer, "Resolute Ignorance: Social Science and Affirmative Action," *Social Science and Public Policy* 24, no. 4 (May/June 1987): 64.

Chapter 7

Mathematical and Scientific Confusion

Confusion infects discussions about education because statistics and scientific findings are often misused. Many believe that this subspecialty of mathematical analysis, statistics, adds heft to a sociological or economic argument. Unfortunately, scholarly tools can misfire as easily as weapons in the wrong hands—or worse, can be deliberately used as such. Let us examine some of the misuses of statistical analysis.

EGREGIOUS MISUSE OF STATISTICS

Consider a simple example dealing with test scores (which are discussed in detail in chapter 9): There are four students, one of whom scores a 90, another who scores a respectable 75, a third who scores a less respectable 70, and a fourth, the outlier, who scores a *zero* (0). The arithmetic average is 58.75 percent, which is lower than all scores except the zero. In addition, the "average" score is failing (assuming 60 is a passing score).

It is clear that the outlier distorts the statistics for all four students. The problem is that simple averages such as this are too often misused for the purpose of scoring political points. For the example, one could have decried the 100 percent failure rate (the average test score was a failing 58.75 percent). Somewhat less apocalyptically, one could have called for drastic measures for "improving the abysmal performance of our schools," even though 75 percent of the students scored between respectable and very well.

This simple example shows that the uncritical acceptance of statistical averages without including variances followed by a careful analysis (that includes error estimates) is fundamentally meaningless. They do not generate wisdom and they cannot be used to solve problems. They are, in fact, a major source of chaos and confusion.

This example also indicates that applying a one-size-fits-all solution to the four "failures" is nonsensical. Of the students surveyed, 75 percent passed the test. And the proposed solution—an increased federal education tax—will drive more students into the home school and for-profit arenas, creating a new and different set of challenges and problems.

As discussed in the previous chapter, one source of confusion in scholarly and policy-making discussions about American public school education is that we are overwhelmed and finally cowed by misreported and bogus statistical studies. These studies are bogus for several concrete reasons:

1. Variances, which are approximate measures of the "width" of the average, are rarely provided.[1]
2. Surveys do not address the underlying problems and instead construct a virtual substitute for policy by posing simple, artificial questions to (random?) persons, such as how they might vote or how they might act when faced with a hypothetical issue. In other words, statistical surveys produce hypothetical answers to hypothetical questions.
3. Statistical studies propose simplistic one-size-fits-all solutions, the consequences of which are often worse than the original problem.
4. Studies are conducted by individuals and organizations with vested interests, many of whom profit greatly by the erroneous solutions that are implemented due to study claims. Their preferred milieu is a state of confusion funded by a vast stream of exploitable public capital.

A common thread in mass-scale statistical prevarication is that the proposed solutions are financial: there are *always* calls for more money and funding.[2] Perhaps even more disturbing, scholarly studies such as that of the late Carol H. Weiss of Harvard University have discussed the fact that "Partisans flourish the evidence in an attempt to neutralize opponents, convince waverers, and bolster supporters (even if) conclusions have to be ripped out of context."[3] Weiss notes also that the biased selection of social science evidence is a viable strategy for advocates of a particular cause, and that it often has a strong policy and political impact. Weiss refers to this practice as "the political model of research utilization," which, in addition to its contributions toward social confusion and discord, is often one of the gateways to personal financial gain.

The remedy to this statistical confusion is, of course, to disaggregate the statistics as carefully as possible so it is clear what is being described, and how. The power of this approach will be demonstrated in chapter 9, when we discuss various careful statistical studies of education.

CARRYING CAPACITY AND BREAKING POINT

Most people have a fairly clear idea of what "bad schools" are like, and why, even if they never articulate it. As a result, the policy pursued by most people is to keep quiet while voting with their feet or running from the problem.

The consequence of running from the problem is that the new neighborhoods and schools temporarily flourish while the older ones decay ever faster as capital and expertise also depart. Why only temporarily? Because this is our pattern of behavior: As a society we are conjoined by a common domestic purpose. Failing schools, like all schools, require upkeep, and therefore continued funding. But because the neighborhoods that house these failing schools (from which many people have already fled) are poorly run and often financially delinquent or even bankrupt, they require for their continued existence the financial support of surrounding well-managed affluent areas, often across an entire state. Eventually, the burden becomes too great, even for the state. Bankruptcy and impoverishment follow, even for those who thought they had escaped.

Consider the case of Detroit. Taxes collected statewide are spent, irresponsibly and corruptly, in the continued support of this blighted city. Many of the tax revenues simply disappeared, as the bankruptcy proceedings in 2014 demonstrated. The emergency financial manager appointed by Governor Rick Snyder (R-MI) in 2013 to oversee Michigan's attempt to render Detroit solvent, Kevyn Orr, uncovered onion-like layers of financial malfeasance and corruption. Their effects will reverberate in Michigan's state budgets for decades.

A solution for Detroit's schools was proposed in 2015 by Governor Snyder, who demanded extensive financial support from the rest of Michigan. In 2016, this initiative was passed, and now these dysfunctional schools will be once again funded to the tune of three-fourths of a billion dollars, although it stretches an already unmanageable budget even further. As this social and educational blight metastasizes, increased financial and social strain is placed on surrounding prosperous, functioning, stable, low-crime neighborhoods.

This practice may continue until a breaking point is reached.[4]

The breaking point is related to what may be called the "carrying capacity" of a society, which is understood by asking a simple question: What is the percentage of dysfunctional individuals or institutions that the remainder of society can support? Is it 5, 50, or 95 percent? Once that carrying capacity is exceeded, civilization may collapse into chaos and anarchy—and order of a degraded kind emerge (think *Mad Max*).

As a simple domestic example of carrying capacity, consider the case of a single family consisting of two parents (2) and three children (3), plus two living grandparents (2), and four aunts and uncles (4). How many family members who are alcoholics, drug addicts, or recidivist criminals can this family of eleven support: two, five, nine, or all eleven? What is that family's carrying capacity? What is its breaking point? The scale of a society is vastly larger than a single family, but when its "elastic response" is exceeded, it will snap.

A heartbreaking account of carrying capacity is the case of former championship-caliber boxer George Chuvalo, whose family of seven once included husband, wife, four sons, and a daughter. The oldest child committed suicide after struggling with heroin addiction. A second son died of a heroin overdose. These two deaths pushed Mrs. Chuvalo beyond her carrying capacity: she reached her breaking point and committed suicide.[5] Sometime later a third son also died of a heroin overdose, making a total of four deaths (57 percent) among seven family members.

Of course, carrying capacity and breaking point need not be as extreme as the Chuvalo example. Many private charities and safety nets have been established for those in need during trying times. One of these safety nets is the Ronald MacDonald House, which helps often single and poor soon-to-be young mothers during and after their delivery. Other organizations, too numerous to mention, reflect a similarly generous, noble sentiment that addresses a real problem: how to care for those closest to us in their times of need. This concern resonates with the human desire to help those we care about, which often includes the stranger (think of the parable of the Good Samaritan).

Calling upon ourselves to care for entire villages, cities, countries, civilizations, or continents, however, may be pushing our carrying capacity past the breaking point, especially when the act of "carrying" is governmentally mandated using the force of taxation coupled to legal sanctions.

HUMAN BIOLOGY

Does talent correlate with biology? People don't like acknowledging this because it runs counter to the American need for level playing fields. President G.W. Bush said it was bigotry to tell someone his abilities appeared in areas other than academics. Many believe that hard viewpoints violate Christian principles. Even here the facts intervene. Mixed in with loving counsel, Jesus uttered many stern statements, including, "Do not scatter good seed on bad ground" and "Go forth and sin no more."

Daily we hear discussions and read articles on "good" and "bad" genes as scientific research propels our knowledge of human life forward. The empirical evidence suggests that biology plays the major role in almost all features of human behavior ranging from the minor (e.g., prevalence of freckles) to the general (psychological character, ability, and inclination).[6] Our confusion stems from our inability to understand and appreciate the degree to which our biological makeup dictates our lives.

MENTAL ACTIVITY

Mental activity can be described as mental horsepower or intelligence or IQ. This produces anxiety among those who believe intelligence testing is the first step toward eugenics. Egalitarianism asserts, absurdly, that "we are all the same," identically abled and equally capable. Denying the importance of biological functions and their centrality in learning (and in all human activities), however, amounts to denying scientific scholarship and evidence. This, too, leads to confusion and unsettlement in society.

One method of assessing cognitive engagement is by asking a question: "How much blood flows to a specific brain region after the person is subjected to various stimuli?" A dye is placed in the subject's blood stream and localized brain function, measured by blood flow into that region, is optically mapped. The technical term for this procedure is "Functional Magnetic Resonance Imaging" (FMRI), which postulates that neurons require more oxygen while being used and relates changes in (measured) local blood flow to neural activity. When the subject is exposed to different stimuli—pain, logical puzzles, aesthetic or erotic images—different segments of the brain will respond with either increased or possibly decreased blood flow. Research shows different responses for men, women as well as adults and children.

Does the amount of blood congregating in a part of the brain determine intelligence, IQ, or what is referred to in psychology as *g*? Not actually, but congregating blood is a quantitative indicator of activity level, which implies greater brain usage and, presumably, greater focus and engagement with the stimulus. The main hypothesis is cause and effect. Studies are likely underway to measure brain-region response between various groups. Quantifiable measures of mental activity across sectors of the population may soon be more than conjecture.

We know there is fast-twitch muscle tissue. Is there fast-twitch gray matter?

We've all encountered people with unique abilities, those who can recite various facts and statistics, for example, or quickly make complicated mathematical calculations without the aid of a calculator, but who are ordinary in other areas of life. Certain parts of their brains appear to be fast-twitch, while others are not. Perhaps the mapping of responses means that the human brain can be viewed not as a single "sponge" but rather as a quilt of sponges, some of which function well for specific tasks (mathematics, empathy, etc.). Certain groups, due to reproduction habits, geography (point of origin), nutrition, and other historical characteristics and consequences, may have larger capacities in one or other specific region of this quilt.

One writer has called the mapping of the brain the "great adventure" of present-day science.[7]

KEY IDEAS

There will never be a science of human behavior that functions at the same level of mathematical precision as physics or chemistry. Eliminating the misuse of statistics and data, and the misrepresentation and misuse of the tools of science would go a long way toward restoring credibility and plausibility to discussions of social policy. This is unlikely however, since graduate students even at top university public policy programs often appear to be more interested in social activism than in using reason and analysis to approach issues and research.

Nevertheless, science marches onward and new evidence of ways of thinking and behaving are being quantified. How long will it be possible to deny that evidence?

NOTES

1. One presidential poll claims that candidate X is ahead of candidate Y by 53 to 42 percent, with 5 percent undecided and a poll margin of error of ± 3 percent (53 ± 1.6, 42 ± 1.26 and 5 ± 0.15). Another poll in the same state claims that Y is ahead of X by 51 to 42 percent, with 7 percent undecided and a poll margin error of ± 2 percent (51 ± 1, 42 ± 0.84 and 7 ± 0.14). There is no overlap in these estimates. One poll shows X strongly ahead, while the other shows Y as the clear winner. The polls cannot be reconciled and so the error estimates are inaccurate. There is obviously either bias in the samples, or the samples are too small, or unrepresentative.

2. On October 9, 2012, *Dianne Rehm Show*, where the panel that discussed public education fully agreed on one issue, the solution to our educational problems was more funding. To see how expenditures have grown, see Lauren Camera, "Federal Education Funding: Where Does the Money Go?" *U.S. News and World Report*, January 14, 2016, https://www.usnews.com/news/blogs/data-mine/2016/01/14/federal-education-funding-where-does-the-money-go.

3. Carol H. Weiss, "The Many Meanings of Research Utilization," *Public Administration Review* 39, no. 5 (September/October 1979): 429.

4. In the case of Atlanta, Georgia, some of the neighboring suburbs have redefined themselves as "cities" in order to halt the expropriation of funds for the continued operation of dysfunctional Atlanta. See Mark Niesse, "New Cities Could Further Split Atlanta Region," *Atlanta Journal-Constitution*, February 21, 2015, http://www.

myajc.com/news/local-govt—politics/new-cities-could-further-split-atlanta-region/ zyP5X5R3PyvQa5BZ8SOsNO/.

5. George Chuvalo, "Memoir: Boxing Champ George Chuvalo Describes His Family's Heartbreaking Battle with Heroin," *Toronto Life*, November 7, 2013, http:// torontolife.com/city/george-chuvalo-memoir/.

6. For a readable layman's discussion of these topics see Nicholas Wade, *A Troublesome Inheritance: Genes, Race and Human History* (New York, Penguin Press, 2014).

7. Tony Rothman, "Searching for Great Adventures," *American Scientist* 102, no. 1 (January–February 2014): 10–13, http://www.americanscientist.org/issues/pub/ searching-for-great-adventures.

Chapter 8

Symptoms and Consequences

As should be clear by this point in the discussion, the consequences of confusion are often dire—for both individual and society. Consider these high-profile cases.

ATLANTA PUBLIC SCHOOL DEBACLE

Circa 2009, hearts were gladdened to learn that Atlanta public schools were improving. Test scores were rising, as shown by quantitative evidence. It was good news at last from a troubled urban region that perpetually languished near the bottom of quantitative indicators of social dysfunction and human misery.

The massive influx of funds directed toward education appeared to produce higher scores on standardized tests. Politicians and economists predicted they would: they always do. Indeed, what could make more sense for budget and economic policy analysts? What could be more affirming for business-minded folks than PowerPoint slides with rising test scores standing beside increased school funds?

Increased budgets met inner-city Atlanta education policy makers and America's heartstrings were tugged. In this worldview, money is funneled into the educational pipeline and high test scores flow out. Here is the mathematical formula for this process:

constant × money (in) = test scores (out)

ALL WE NEED TO DO NOW IS TO CALIBRATE
THE *CONSTANT* ON THE LEFT-HAND SIDE
OF THE EQUATION

Sadly, Atlanta's public school reality proved otherwise. The money pipeline equation mentioned earlier did not describe Atlanta's social experiment in public education. Large sums were indeed funneled into the educational pipeline and "money (in)" increased—a lot. But the test scores on the right-hand side of the equation *did not* increase. In fact the test scores stayed constant, or decreased.

The truth of the Atlanta scandal was that the alleged and much publicized rise of the test scores was a fraud perpetrated upon Peach State taxpayers. Atlanta schoolchildren performed as they always had: substantially below their statewide counterparts.

How did they do so well on those tests? After a criminal investigation, about forty Atlanta school teachers and administrators were arraigned on charges of fraud, racketeering, and corruption.[1] They had provided correct answers to students beforehand and falsified test results. Test scores had not risen, the public schools were still awful, Atlanta's schoolchildren still underperformed relative to the rest of the Peach State, and honesty went missing.

What about the left-hand side of the equation? Where did all the money taken from the paychecks of Georgia's (and America's) taxpayers go, if not to increase test scores? As the evidence continues to mount, it seems likely that it went into circulation, though certainly not where intended.[2] The Atlanta education renewal program was a twisting of the truth, an unsavory morsel of corruption, venality, and greed. A societal problem was once again "solved" by carelessly spending enormous sums of taxpayer money on it.

Unfortunately, instead of fitting Atlanta's students with a viable educational pipeline, a greed-corruption-graft pipeline for "community leaders" and "educators" was installed. Atlanta's public schools employed more than forty teachers and administrators, partners in crime, who were sufficiently jaded by the dismal condition of their inner-city schools to participate, willingly, even eagerly, in this fraud, which took the *apparently* sensible form of budget increases meant to produce higher test scores (the equation for success).

This plan was set in motion by the administrators and bureaucrats who, playing on their fellow Georgians' compassion—who can say "no" to educating our wonderful children?—tied school performance to per-pupil spending and fully funded extra assistance programs. It was widely asserted that Head Start and related programs, including free breakfast and lunch for students, correlated with improved test scores.[3] These were bogus claims, but the Peach State taxpayers funded all of it.

High test scores were "achieved" by deceit and cheating, not by legitimate student accomplishment. Honesty—the marriage of the ideal with the real— was the first casualty in this squalid enterprise.

DYSFUNCTIONAL SCHOOLS HAVE SOMETHING IN COMMON

Confusion about all of the issues discussed in this book appears in countless school districts in at least three forms: (1) the scale of financial mismanagement by local citizenry and officialdom; (2) the spectacularly poor performance of its students; and (3) the response of parents, presiding officials, and media.

Excuses abound. A laid-off teacher in Highland Park, Michigan, argues that her school district's problems are "not entirely" the fault of the neighborhood: "The disinvestment in our communities led to the disinvestment in our schools, and that's why people left. We had nothing to offer them."[4] Nothing to offer them? Despite a funding rate, almost 80 percent higher than an already high average value in the state of Michigan?

Not taking responsibility is a glaringly obvious symptom of prevailing social dysfunction in these communities.

How would the teacher cited earlier in the text explain why his or her school and similarly underperforming schools cost nearly twice as much per pupil to operate as other schools across the state? A significant part of the funding, as has been often argued, is often lost to corruption, misuse, and theft.

The journalist David Keene writes that "Maryland, like Illinois, is famous as an integrity-free zone. Former governors, the heads of various school systems in the state, legislators, county executives and law enforcement officials have ended their careers in federal and state penal institutions for confusing serving the public with serving themselves at the public's expense." He adds that "Prince George's County just outside Washington and across the Wilson Bridge from Alexandria has probably had more former elected and appointed officials incarcerated than any other state jurisdiction, including Baltimore. . . . The county's political culture is toxic to those who believe that elected officials should resist the temptation to steal from those who elect them, and it is a culture that seems eternally resistant to reform. It's a shame, because the historic picturesque county should be a great place to live and raise a family."

Keene also notes accurately that "Prince George's is not a poor county by any measure, but audits of their school system have revealed that much of the money earmarked for education is wasted or stolen. Maybe that's why at least one former head of the system went to prison for public corruption. Still, the county executive claims the county is broke and needs help either from the state or in the form of much higher taxes."[5]

Illegitimacy and fatherlessness compounds the problem, as shown in table 4.1 in chapter 4. A large proportion of the local single mothers are simply too young to be responsible parents. They receive generous government assistance such as food stamps and Electronic Benefits Transfer (EBT) on a per-child basis, for the tax incentives written into the U.S. tax code distill to a very simple result: more children → more aid.

Tendencies toward antisocial behavior are exacerbated, since the children in troubled neighborhoods are often born to mothers with poor life habits and skills, and little education. In the worst cases, they smoke, drink large quantities of alcohol, and often use street drugs, leaving their children to wander about on the streets foraging for food.[6] Many of these children are born with an addiction to drugs that began in their mother's womb.

At home and in the community, these children and their family members speak a variant of English, which has recently been labeled Ebonics. The scholarly evidence suggests that the absence of books and the baneful influence of television, compounded by the lack of education of parents or caregivers, affect the children's ability to speak and write Standard English. This shows an even greater need for basic skills.

Nevertheless, whether Ebonics is encouraged or not, it seems impossible to graft good schools onto the troubled neighborhoods that contain the households described here, no matter how outstanding the teachers or how costly and modern the facilities. Reform must begin with the people of these neighborhoods. It is best for children to be raised in a two-parent household (again, see the data in table 4.1 in chapter 4). High-involvement parenting should be taught, encouraged, and practiced. In terms of education, this means spending time with a child, monitoring homework, providing a good study environment, and attending parent-teacher conferences.

Such behaviors must be incentivized along with marriage and all other forms of social stability. Deleterious incentives for illegitimacy, unemployment, and delinquency must be eliminated, and bogus educational programming exposed. The culture of easy materialism and public assistance has been a half-century "Great Society" millstone around the necks of ordinary Americans. What ostensibly began as "assistance" has devolved into a deplorable condition of multigenerational dependence.

KEY IDEAS

What are the consequences of mass educational and societal confusion? Statistics indicate that America's social problems have grown steadily worse as illegitimacy, crime, and dysfunctional behavior and reasoning are rewarded at ever-higher rates of return.

In July 2014, a morning discussion on FM radio 90.5 WKAR in East Lansing, Michigan, centered on Lansing mayor Virgil "Virg" Bernero's self-proclaimed "new initiatives on community development." His focus was on getting dysfunctional "families of color" (Bernero's words) to behave responsibly, attend school, and eschew teenage pregnancy. Has this not been our focus since the mid-1960s? Why are we still facing the same issues and proposing the same "solutions"?

What has been wrought may be, at least partially, undone (or redeemed) if incentives for good behavior are implemented and the mistaken policies of the past are abandoned. What must be avoided, if such steps are not implemented, is the slowly growing demoralization and cynicism over these issues among Americans, most of whom try to live and work honestly. When *Weltschmerz*—a dejected world-weariness—becomes the norm, social amity, societal tranquility, and the well-being of posterity are in peril.

NOTES

1. This details of this scandal have been extensively analyzed, though not in the mainstream media. The principal culprit, Beverly Hall, superintendent of Atlanta schools, was named the 2009 "Superintendent of the Year." Under her watch and with the collaboration of the almost all-white Atlanta Chamber of Commerce, the goal was to make Atlanta attractive for business investment (again, see the "formula for success"). See the exposé by Heather Vogell, "July 2011: Report Says Suspected Wrongdoing Could Lead to Criminal Charges for Some," AJC.com, July 26, 2011, http://www.ajc.com/news/local/july-2011-report-says-suspected-wrongdoing-could-lead-criminal-charges-for-some/bX4bEZDWbeOH33cDkod1FL/,which reveals the extent of the corruption.

2. When assessing a region's affluence, it makes the most sense to measure local expenditures, not local incomes. These two numbers are often dramatically unequal. In America's so-called poorest neighborhoods, the former is often far larger than the latter, indicating that, there is money in the neighborhood, the source of which cannot be determined.

3. Impartial, quantitative analysis of statistics shows that these programs do not produce any measurable increase in student performance. What they actually amount to is taxpayer-funded childcare. This has been pointed out in scholarly studies such as Lips, Watkins, and Fleming, *Does Spending More on Education Improve Academic Achievement?* The authors of this study note that spending on public education rose between 1970 and 2005 from $4,060 to $9,270 per pupil per year (in 2006–2007 dollars), while test scores, graduation rates among groups (white, black), and reading and mathematics "gaps" have remained the same. Education scholar Eric A. Hanushek is quoted on page 5:

> Few people . . . would recommend just dumping extra resources into existing schools. America has . . . followed that program for several decades, with no sign that student performance has improved.

This issue is getting productive uses from current and added spending. The existing evidence simply indicates that the typical school system does not use resources well (at least if promoting student achievement is their purpose).

In an understatement, Lips and co-authors assert that "policymakers should seriously consider improving how to allocate educational resources more effectively." (6)

4. Quoted in Banchero and Dolan, "Highland Park Turns over Troubled Operations."

5. David Keene, "When the Problem Isn't Revenue but Out-of-Control Spending," *Washington Times*, Wednesday, July 22, 2015, http://www.washingtontimes.com/news/2015/jul/22/david-keene-big-government-can-never-have-enough-m/.

6. Theodore Dalrymple, *Life at the Bottom: The Worldview That Makes the Underclass* (Chicago: Ivan R. Dee, 2001).

Chapter 9

Facts about Education

The empirical evidence must weigh heavily in the planning of educational objectives and approaches. Mountains of data have accumulated even as mountains more are being gathered. Unfortunately, many among us are unaware of the empirical data, and some choose to ignore or even suppress it. Such individuals base their choices on intuition, anecdote, or their beliefs about the way the world *should be*.[1]

We have to find a balance, a way to unite evidence with objective.

In *Greek Science in Antiquity*, the late Marshall Clagett notes that "the growth of modern science (which is based on the classical Greek conception of the rational universe) . . . has been brought about . . . largely . . . by the development of experimental ways to establish the surety and firmness of manifold bonds that unite theory and experience."[2] We require theories united with observation and experience, the latter being understood as practical knowledge of the world gleaned by living, watching, and synthesizing, in order to increase our store of knowledge, especially for the inexact sciences.

For example, Lloyd L. Withrow, head of General Motors Fuels and Lubricants research and development, from its inception until 1962 dealt with important technical issues in automobiles sold worldwide. Without suitable fuels and lubricants, automobiles may cause accidents and other catastrophes (e.g., fires). Withrow's philosophy: "Let the data tell you what the answer is."[3] Doing the opposite—distorting the data to fit preconceived or erroneous notions may lead to compounded problems and even professional disgrace.[4] Like Withrow, we should let our mountains of data tell us what the answers are to the problems of American public K–12 education.

But as much as we know from living, much more information exists that has been gathered, recorded, and assessed, and it lies at our fingertips. The previous chapters have weighed heavily on observation, example, and anecdote. Here we focus on some of the serious scholarly research on education that supports my thesis that a one-size-fits-all approach to public K–12 education is guaranteed to (continue to) fail.

IRREPRESSIBLE FACTS

The taxonomy of this book addresses two groups of students in America.

The first group is the upper tier, or roughly the top fiftieth percentile of students, most of whom will benefit to varying degrees from an academic education of the kind that has prevailed for the past century. Some in this group will merely get by. Only the truly upper-fraction, about one-fifth of this group, is capable of producing outstanding academic work.

The second group is the lower tier, or lower 50th percentile (see figure 1.1 in chapter 1), comprises the decently diligent who do not possess the requisite ability to succeed in pure academics. (Dropouts are not counted among the top or bottom 50 percent, since they no longer seek an education. Some of the dropout rate would consist of troubled youth, who would comprise a third group, called "the dysfunctional," and who in the past were tracked to reform school or juvenile incarceration.)

The focus of a revamped system of K–12 public education should be placed on this second group of students, who absorb tremendous community and financial resources with little tangible benefit. These students should more accurately be called the differently educable. After about eighth grade, the mountains of data have shown, the differently educable display little interest/aptitude/talent in academic subjects and abstract and conceptual pursuits. For these students, an academic education from eighth through twelfth grade is largely a misuse of our finite educational resources.

In my proposed system, the principal function of an elementary school would be to determine who is academically educable and who is differently educable. The elementary school would teach academic and nonacademic students the basics of history, civics, as much mathematics as they can handle, and a variety of subjects including art, music, and physical education, that they can absorb.

In middle school, a final effort would be made to provide the differently educable the basics of history, language, and mathematics, among other subjects, to the extent of their ability to learn these subjects. This is the point where the focus of the two group's educations begins to diverge as students are sorted into sections, each learning a curriculum based on his or her differing abilities. The issues of late bloomers and of crossover between academic and nonacademic programs, always a sensitive subject, are not covered in this book.

STATISTICAL ANALYSES OF AMERICAN MIDDLE AND HIGH SCHOOL ACADEMIC EDUCATION

In the tests discussed here, K–12 students were required to solve abstract pencil-and-paper intellectual puzzles. They also read and criticized essays of various degrees of complexity. The results are interesting.

Pencil-and-paper academic testing has been shown to be valuable for assessing subsequent academic performance at the university level as well as to be a reasonably reliable predictor of career success in current prestige fields.[5] This method of testing has not been valuable for differently educable students except as a means for filtering them out of the more difficult academic programs.

These assessments can often be made relatively early in a student's life. On the other hand, pencil-and-paper testing is not useful past a certain age except as an indicator either of stasis (scores remain constant over the years, indicating that the students are on the right track and their learning is proceeding apace) or of decline (scores drop over the years, indicating that the additional time spent in school has been fruitless and they did better, relatively speaking, in their earlier grades).

When analyzing actual metadata, it is important to deploy careful statistical analyses. What follows is a discussion of important preliminary analyses of the academic test scores of American and international middle and high school students. I use *preliminary* because these sorts of analyses, which use statistical methods of data disaggregation, are only now becoming more common. The Boe-Shin study of American educational testing and outcomes described next is among the first studies of educational testing results to disaggregate the metadata.

THE BOE-SHIN STUDY

The test scores of American high school students have been gathered over many years, in some cases, decades, and evaluated in various comprehensive international comparisons such as the Reading Literacy Study, which provides internationally comparative data about students' reading achievement in the fourth grade in most participating countries; the Third International Mathematics and Science Study (TIMSS), which, for example, in 2011 examined fourth- and eighth-grade student achievement in sixty-three countries; and the Civic Educational Study (CES), which periodically surveys between 100,000 and 150,000 fourteen-year-old students in approximately 30–40 countries (see http://research.acer.edu.au/civics/5/).

In their excellent article on these studies, "Is the United States Really Losing the International Horse Race in Academic Achievement?" Erling E. Boe and Sujie Shin of the University of Pennsylvania begin by quoting those who have alleged that the scores of American students are "mediocre" compared with other industrialized nations (Western G5 plus Japan, or the G7, which consists of Canada, France, Germany, Italy, Japan, the United Kingdom, and the United States, countries that represent over 50 percent of net global wealth).[6] Americans perform "poorly"; there is a "pervasive and intolerable mediocrity in mathematics teaching"; "many" nations score "better than" U.S. students.[7] Boe and Shin mention the National Commission on Excellence in Education's 1983 study, *A Nation at Risk: The Imperative for Educational Reform*, which asserts that "on 19 academic tests American students were never first or second and, in comparison with other industrialized nations, were last seven times."[8]

The trouble, Boe and Shin point out, is that these damning statistics are customarily analyzed by making blanket comparisons between countries with little in common, between peoples and circumstances with little in common, and between educational systems with little in common. Boe and Shin observe that the perception of poor performance of American students in international comparisons is "typically attributed to the ineffectiveness of public education." (See the discussion on teacher-bashing in chapter 2.) And since public education is ineffective, educators "and policy makers . . . embrace this conclusion because it creates enormous pressure for change."[9]

These changes, which Boe and Shin should have referred to as "tweaks" to the existing system, involve financial incentives such as new books and "teaching tools," including expensive computer hardware and software. There is a strong vested financial interest in proclaiming poor test scores and then proposing expensive remedies. This tactic was discussed in chapter 2.

Boe and Shin disaggregated the data and fine-tuned their comparisons. Their results revealed details and subtleties unavailable in the global data. Why is that? Because global averages muddy the complex structure of the data by smoothing over important details. Even though the global average values are correct, interpreting those averages is difficult to do, which leads to alarmist interpretations and statements. After being barraged by hyperbolic negativism, the American public is ripe for taxpayer-funded educational initiatives.

An example much discussed in these pages is the DPS. With chronic problems and poor performance, with competency rates hovering in the single digits in reading and mathematics for DPS graduates, with the worst academic performance of America's major cities, and despite ample evidence of corruption and incompetence across all levels of its administration, DPS will be funded $750 million for the next several years. These funds, gathered from the rest of Michigan, will presumably get DPS "on the right track," making them "feasible" by "eliminating funding and resource inequalities" and assuring that Detroit students "have a chance."

In their tables and charts, Boe and Shin show the following points:

1. Overall or average American test scores, compared with those of the other industrialized countries (such as the G7), were neither mediocre nor abysmal. In fact, they were slightly above average. Before making this comparison, Boe and Shin discussed why it makes no sense to compare the United States (population somewhere between 325–350 million) with countries such as Finland and Singapore (populations smaller than most American states). Boe and Shin asserted that the proper basis for comparison is other large, wealthy industrial countries.

2. American children can be divided into groups by grade level, race, and sex. Boe and Shin focused on racial groups self-identifying as white, Asian (probably Indian and Chinese), black, and Hispanic. After disaggregating the global statistics along racial lines, features emerged that were not apparent in the global numbers.

3. White and Asian children and young adults (high school students) scored near the top of the international group. Only the Japanese fared slightly better than the top Americans. In other words, the U.S. whites and Asians performed at the highest level of these wealthy industrial countries of the world.

4. Black and Hispanic children performed at the bottom of the international rankings. Their scores were so low that when this much smaller group (20 to 30 percent the size of the white/Asian group) was averaged with the white/Asian cohort, the resulting scores nosedived from among the very highest to upper-middle-of-the-pack. This is not a bad placement among the world's most powerful and prosperous countries, but it is low compared with children whose test scores place them at the top of this distinguished group of countries.

5. Boe and Shin concluded:

   A major impediment to higher average achievement scores in the United States is the performance of its black and Hispanic students. The achievement gap goes back decades and is not closing rapidly (if at all). Moreover, demographic trends exacerbate the impact of the achievement gap on U.S. mean achievement scores. In 1991, the population of the public school students was 70 percent white and 26 percent black and Hispanic. By the year 2000, black and Hispanic students represented about 34 percent of the student population, a stunning growth of 8 percent of the total during a ten-year period (or growth of nearly

1 percent per year). If the achievement gap remains constant, we can predict that U.S. mean scores will decline as the minority population increases as a percentage of the total.[10]

6. Finally, on a positive note, Boe and Shin assert that "in recent years, the U.S. has not performed 'poorly' in international comparisons in a statistical sense. Consequently, an allegation of poor performance should not be used to tarnish the constructive work of the majority of public educators and the genuine attainments of U.S. students."[11]

This book is not the place to make detailed comparisons, because Boe and Shin have done that. Their well-written public domain article is accessible on the Internet. Boe said in 2014 that it is being downloaded once per day, a high rate for a scholarly article. (A more extensive version of this same study is available as an internal University of Pennsylvania Center for Research and Evaluation in Social Policy research report.)[12] It is clear from the Boe and Shin study that a large cohort of American students (white, Asian) is doing quite well, whereas a large and rapidly growing cohort (Hispanic, black) is doing very poorly.

Boe and Shin do not discuss it, but it appears that an improved paradigm is needed to educate the low-performing students, no matter their group. It is clear that the trouble lies in the bottom 50 percent, a disproportionate segment of which, Boe and Shin show, consists of specific racial and ethnic minorities. On the flip side, a disproportionate share of different minorities comprises the top-scoring segment.

THE CARNOY-ROTHSTEIN STUDY

Data disaggregation is the core analytical feature of "What Do International Tests Really Show about U.S. Student Performance?" a major study published in early 2013 by the Economic Policy Institute.[13] The disaggregation criterion used by study authors Martin Carnoy and Richard Rothstein is number of books in household (BH), because comparing international data is difficult when using either monetary data or self-identified race or ethnicity. Carnoy and Rothstein state that a reasonable way to distinguish between social class groups across countries is by BH, with BH < 10 denoting disadvantaged; $11 \leq BH \leq 25$ denoting slightly less disadvantaged; $26 \leq BH \leq 100$ and 101–200 denoting more-or-less neutrally advantaged; and 201–500 and >500 denoting advantaged.[14]

Carnoy and Rothstein arrive at approximately the same conclusions as Boe and Shin. The United States is not performing poorly: low-BH students in America perform better than low-BH students in other countries. When underperforming low-BH students are removed from the data, the disaggregated U.S. results are impressive and significantly—in the statistical sense—higher than results for economic powerhouses such as Germany and England. They also compare well with small, efficient countries such as Canada and Finland. Canada's population is 10 percent smaller than California's; Finland's population is slightly more than half of Michigan's.

Carnoy and Rothstein evaluated changes in test scores over time. In many cases, the rate of improvement of low-BH households is higher than in other post industrial countries. In some countries, the improvement rate is negative. For this reason, Carnoy and Rothstein indicate that administrators should not merely use absolute numbers but should carefully consider rates of change in order to retain policies that are working.[15]

Finally, and most disconcertingly, the authors found that the high-BH trends move mostly in the wrong direction, that is, their scores are declining over time, relatively. The scores are still high, but no longer as high: "U.S. policy discussion assumes that most of the problems of the U.S. education system are concentrated in schools serving disadvantaged children. Trends in PISA scores suggest that the opposite may be true."[16] In other words, we are spending so much time and effort (and money) on low-BH children and we are neglecting the much more academic high-BH children.

Following are some of the most salient points Carnoy and Rothstein make in their extremely thorough analysis:

1. Statements to the effect that U.S. education is failing when compared with the international competition are "oversimplified, frequently exaggerated, and misleading. They ignore the complexity of test results and may lead policymakers to pursue inappropriate and even harmful reforms."
2. The "U.S. average performance appears to be relatively low partly because we have so many test takers from the bottom of the social class distribution." (Carnoy and Rothstein's data show that among postindustrial countries, the United States has by far the largest cohort of low-BH students.)
3. "If U. S. adolescents had a social class distribution that was similar to the distributions in countries to which the United States is frequently compared, average reading scores in the United States would be higher than average reading scores in the similar post industrial countries we examined (France, Germany, and the United Kingdom), and average math scores in the United States would be about the same as average math scores in similar post industrial countries."
4. "We are certain of this: To make judgments only on the basis of statistically significant differences in national average scores on only one test, at only one point in time, without regard to social class context or population

sampling methodologies, is the worst possible choice. But, unfortunately, this is how most policymakers and analysts approach the field."[17]

THE LADNER-MYSLINSKI STUDY

In *Report Card on American Education: Ranking State K–12 Performance, Progress, and Reform* (2013), the (eighteenth) annual report on the status of American K–12 education, authors Matthew Ladner and David Myslinski of the Foundation for Excellence in Education state that America's "system of schooling continues to systematically underserve" our "low-income and minority students, despite large, above-and-beyond increases in per-pupil spending."[18]

In agreement with Boe and Shin, Ladner and Myslinski state, "American 15-year old white students score at an internationally competitive level, but one can only describe the results for black and Hispanic students as catastrophic." These students "fail to learn basic literacy skills in the developmentally critical grades" and rather than "addressing these problems head-on, standard practice involves simply promoting students to the next grade" (recall education "option 3" in chapter 1 and the example of Dasmine Cathay discussed in chapter 2). Ladner and Myslinski describe this as a "crisis and a source of enormous national shame." Moreover, the "collective failure of American schools and society to educate low-income and minority students has produced . . . a 'permanent national recession' in America."[19] Thus, poor performance in a conventional school setting carries practical, economic implications for this grossly underperforming cohort.

While Ladner and Myslinski offer extended discussions of both the "White-Black Achievement Gap" and the "White-Hispanic Achievement Gap," certain gaps in various tests appear to be closing. Other trends are more worrisome. For example, Ladner and Myslinski are troubled by the "geological rate of progress" in closing these gaps. They point to the challenges minority groups face, with Hispanics, in particular, often wrestling with "language barriers" that Ladner and Myslinski "hope" are largely responsible for the gap.[20]

Pointing out that the "average American school, district and state did precious little to narrow race-or-income-based achievement gaps between 2003 and 2011," Ladner and Myslinski note that "a disturbingly large swath of schools, districts, and states, in fact, did precisely the opposite," and conclude: "Whatever it is we are doing as a nation to improve the education [of our children] to date, it has not been enough."[21]

SUMMARY OF BOE-SHIN, CARNOY-ROTHSTEIN, AND LADNER-MYSLINSKI

It is illogical to compare the test scores and results for large, industrial powerhouse nations with small, quasi-homogeneous countries (Denmark, Norway, Finland, Singapore, New Zealand), or for that matter to "intermediate" countries (Canada, Australia, Taiwan) that are smaller than many individual American states. Comparisons make sense only for countries of similar size and socioeconomic profile. Tiny and intermediate countries can implement policies, enforce standardization, and generate results at rates that are impossible for a large country like the United States.[22] In addition:

1. Disaggregation of the data is necessary for detecting the subtle structure of the global data (Boe-Shin, Carnoy-Rothstein). Global averages are crude, difficult to interpret, and likely not useful for deciding specific policy issues. Policy makers should be trained in the proper interpretation and understanding of the statistics of large data, including especially the evaluation of rates of change.
2. The upper cohort of American students is doing very well in international comparisons, placing at or near the top (Boe-Shin). Only the Japanese scored better than the top American cohort.
3. The lower cohort of students is doing very poorly in absolute terms (Boe-Shin), although America's lower 50 percent does much better than native cohorts in countries with the same ethnic/racial background (see discussion in the "Good Academics" section in chapter 1). Thus, black students in the United States perform better than black students in other countries. The same is true of Hispanic students, although both American blacks and Hispanics underperform considerably compared with white and Asian American students.
4. There is a distinct racial/ethnic performance gap in education that cannot be ignored (Boe-Shin). This gap does not appear for other racial/ethnic groups such as Chinese, Japanese, Indian, and Pakistani students. The reverse appears to be true as these groups often outperform white Americans.
5. When the upper cohort is averaged with the lower cohort, the resulting global average score indicates mediocrity (Boe-Shin, Carnoy-Rothstein, Ladner-Myslinski). The result—strict middle-of-the-pack overall performance—is criticized as being unacceptable when the statistics are released to the media and the political establishment.
6. The number of underperforming students in the United States is rapidly increasing both by natural reproduction and immigration (Boe-Shin,

Carnoy-Rothstein). In other words, students some of whom are American citizens and others who are immigrants are adding rapidly to the overall number of underperforming students.

7. The rate of improvement of the lower cohort is greater than that of the upper cohort (Carnoy-Rothstein). The rate of improvement of the upper cohort is negative, meaning that the upper cohort is performing worse on tests than it has done in the past. In other words, the trend is downward (Carnoy-Rothstein).

8. Testing gaps are not closing (Boe-Shin, Carnoy-Rothstein, Ladner-Myslinski). Even as they close for some tests, the overall gaps are not closing. In other words, as the gaps close in a few categories, or on some tests, they widen in others. This trend has persisted for over a century in the United States (and elsewhere) and, according to some researchers, may be tied to biology and inheritance (nature) more than training, diligence, and preparation (nurture). The gaps in test scores are discussed in chapters 10–12.

SUGGESTIONS FOR ADDRESSING/REVERSING THESE TRENDS?

1. Focus academic tests on the academically capable and make international comparisons using that student group. This will be a better indicator of the performance of American academic education. Of course, since every student is being academically educated in fourth grade or earlier, this statement does not apply to that age cohort.

2. In domestic comparisons, disaggregate the data by state and compare individual states with one another, making all attempts to compare like with like, including similar state size, state geography and location, ethnic and racial composition, and so forth.

3. In international comparisons, disaggregate that data and compare countries whose size, geography, ethnic/racial compositions, and so on match various American states. California may be compared with Canada, for example, Michigan with Belgium, Massachusetts with Sweden or Denmark, and Minnesota with Finland.

4. In larger international comparisons, observe that clusters of states such as New York (20 million), Massachusetts (6.5 million), Connecticut (4 million), New Jersey (9 million), and Pennsylvania (13 million) have a total population (53 million) that is identical to that of England, with moderately overlapping demographics. Credible comparisons can be made between England and America's New England.

5. Address the titanic expense involved in the misguided effort at academically educating the lower cohort of American K–12 students. The

commendable goal of improving this student cohort comes at a huge expense, as American public schools are the world's most expensive. Although lower cohort performance has increased marginally (recall that the gaps remain essentially unchanged), these students' scores are more easily raised; it is easier to improve the mediocre performer because there is vast room for improvement. Conversely, it is easier to degrade the performance of the top cohort, which appears to be the case for American K–12 public education.

6. America should direct resources toward practical, achievable goals for the lower cohort of students, because in the end, their test scores are the manifestation of a hard fact about human nature, that in any group of people, about half will be below average and half above average in any measurable level of ability, talent, or skill. While Carnoy and Rothstein produce unimpeachable evidence that the test scores of the lower cohort have improved, these scores are still low (Boe-Shin, Ladner-Myslinski). In fact, the lower cohort's scores are so low that including them with the top cohort produces middle-of-the-pack averages (Boe-Shin). Ladner and Myslinski are less optimistic, instead using words such as "abysmal," "disturbing," and "catastrophic."

REAL-WORLD EXPERIENCE

This section is based on my thirty years of classroom teaching at a Carnegie Research I university.

Nearly all undergraduate classes contain a lower-performing cohort, which comprises, almost without exception, approximately 20 to 30 percent of the final class enrollment.[23] For purposes of discussion, an estimate of approximately 25 percent is reasonable.

Four explanations (any combination therewith) may characterize the presence of this low-performing cohort in class: (1) they dislike the course (*instructor fault*: the instructor makes the class uncomfortable or is a poor teacher); (2) they are ill-prepared for the course (*prior instructor and program fault*: the student was not told that various material was important to the current course, for which the student is therefore ill-prepared); (3) they are unsuited for the course (*personal fault*: the student is insufficiently talented); (4) the institution discriminates against particular types of students (*institutional fault*: society is responsible for the student's failures).

Unsuited and ill-matched students quickly see that they do not have the ability to succeed in the class. They lose interest as they fall further behind. They blame the instructor for their failures. These factors cause a cascade toward a strongly negative impression of the course, possibly their major and the school, and even the larger society, which has "disadvantaged" and "unprivileged" them. This cascade is accompanied by equally strong negative evaluations of the instructor, the course, the major, and the university.

Since there are also many good students in school, let us also consider the traits these students share. The good, successful student is intelligent and motivated, since having the one trait without the other rarely yields success. Such a student asks questions, is humble, and has a desire for knowledge in a chosen field, no matter how quirky, that is unquenchable. He does his homework and attends review sessions, although he may not need them. Such a student only requires guidance and direction, because he loves learning.

Of course, those who love to learn also engage in nonacademic subjects, and no matter what the specialty, the learner learns with a consuming passion.

By contrast, bad academic performance is usually justified through a series of excuses. Some examples from students are "life issues," including "dating troubles," "involvement in athletics," and the need to work "to support myself." Excuses for poor performance, no matter how credible, are an indicator of flagging interest.

One component of academic success or failure is preparation. Another is a student's current circumstances and relationships—do they support studying? Other components are interest and passion, and, perhaps most important, talent. We tend to involve ourselves most successfully in activities in which we have discernible natural ability.

My many years of teaching undergraduates have shown me that roughly 25 percent of every class is not suited to pursue academics, at least not mechanical engineering. These students display little or no intellectual curiosity and would be better served pursuing practical career options that require technical, for example, rather than intensive academic preparation.

A healthy, prosperous country requires the spectrum of skilled contributions of all of it citizens, not only those who are academically trained. These students, the 25 percent, products of K–12 education, should have been educated more appropriately and suitably during their formative years. They would have chosen career pursuits consistent with their talents and interests and would never have appeared in engineering and other demanding academic classes in the first place.

KEY IDEAS

Regardless of the measure used to distinguish excellent from mediocre learners, these empirical studies demonstrate that even though America does well by its underperformers, they still underperform their countrymen. And their low scores on standardized tests lead to mediocre middle-of-the-pack American global averages. Another troubling fact is that the American contingent of underperformers (again, independent of how this is measured) is large and growing, which portends ill for posterities' prosperity and calls for a more sensible, realistic approach to educating our academic underperformers. Once more, this implies that our current one-size-fits-all K–12 public education system must be carefully and thoughtfully retooled.

NOTES

1. This sentence is a rough paraphrase of a comment in David Z. Hambrick and Christopher Chabris, "Yes, IQ Really Matters: Critics of the SAT and Other Standardized Testing Are Disregarding the Data," *Slate*, April 14 2014, http://www.slate.com/articles/health_and_science/science/2014/04/what_do_sat_and_iq_tests_measure_general_intelligence_predicts_school_and.html.

2. Marshall Clagett, *Greek Science in Antiquity* (New York: Abelard-Schuman, 1955; New York: Dover Publications, 2001), 29.

3. J.M. Colucci, "The GMR-GM R&D Fuels and Lubricants Department—Its History and Accomplishments," SAE Technical Paper 2016–01–0176, April 5, 2016, http://papers.sae.org/2016-01-0176/.

4. Stephen J. Gould, evolutionary biologist and popularizer of biological research, accused an 1800s researcher of racism and data falsification. Gould was subsequently found to have falsified data himself in order to force it to comport with his ideas about "social justice," political ideology, and civilizational stereotyping.

5. Cochran and Harpending, *10,000 Year Explosion.*

6. Erling E. Boe and Sujie Shin, "Is the United States Really Losing the International Horse Race in Academic Achievement?" *Phi Delta Kappan* 86, no. 9 (May 2005): 688–95, available at http://repository.upenn.edu/cgi/viewcontent.cgi?article=1004&context=gse_pubs.

7. See Hanushek, Peterson, and Woessmann, "Achievement Growth: International and U. S. Trend in Student Performance," where we find the statement "only 6 percent of U. S. students performed at the advanced level in mathematics, a percentage lower than those attained by 30 other countries." See also William H. Schmidt, "At the Precipice: The Story of Mathematics Education in the U.S.," *Peabody Journal of Education*, 87, no. 1 (January 2012): 133–56. The "realistic appraisal of the NAEP gives grounds for alarm" and many statistics indicate that America has twelfth graders who "ranked near the bottom of all countries in mathematics literacy." This article discusses global statistics averaged over all students, making no distinctions, no disaggregation. Thus, the averaged results are dismal. The section on "Public Support for Challenging Content Standards" indicates that large swaths of the American public misunderstand the role and nature of high school mathematics education: 84 percent of parents queried believed their children should take advanced mathematics classes, and 80 percent believed "mathematics achievement had more to do with education than with native ability" (151).

8. Boe and Shin, "Is the United States Really Losing?" 689, citing *A Nation at Risk: The Imperative for Educational Reform* (Washington, DC: National Commission on Excellence in Education, 1983), 9.

9. Ibid.

10. Ibid., 694.

11. Ibid., 695.

12. Erling E. Boe and Sujie S. Shin, *Is the United States Winning or Losing the International Horse Race in Academic Achievement? Neither—It Is Running with Other Western G7 Nations*, research report No. 2004TIMSS1 (Philadelphia: Center for Research and Evaluation in Social Policy, Graduate School of Education, University of Pennsylvania, 2004), http://www.gse.upenn.edu/cresp/pdfs/RR1-MSS3%20(pdf).pdf.

13. Martin Carnoy and Richard Rothstein, "What Do International Tests Really Show about U.S. Student Performance?" Economic Policy Institute, January 13, 2013, http://www.epi.org/publication/us-student-performance-testing/. This extensive report contains a wealth of information about educational test scores and their implications.

14. As an aside, the BH metric may in many cases represent a preference issue rather than an affordability issue. Consider that one can walk or take a bus for a few dollars, maybe for free, to a local bookstore and purchase, for less than the price of admission to a movie with drink and popcorn, several volumes of Shakespeare's plays and celebrated poetry.

15. It would be necessary for a student majoring in education to take and pass a calculus course to understand a rate of change.

16. Carnoy and Rothstein, "What Do International Tests Really Show?" 83.

17. Ibid.

18. Matthew Ladner and David Myslinski, *Report Card on American Education: Ranking State K–12 Performance, Progress, and Reform*, 18th ed. (Washington, DC: American Legislative Council, 2013), 18, available at https://www.slideshare.net/ALEC_states/132293362-reportcardonamericaneducationrankingstatek12performanceprogressandreform.

19. Ibid., all quotes in this paragraph are taken from p. 20.

20. Ibid., 21–23.

21. Ibid., 33.

22. Several tiny Nordic countries such as Denmark, Finland, Norway, Iceland, and the Baltic countries (Estonia, Latvia, Lithuania) have smaller populations than individual *counties* in the United States.

23. A percentage of students drop the course before the drop period ends. These students are not counted in the tally, hence the fraction of underperforming students may be higher than indicated.

Chapter 10

Clearing Up Social Confusion

Reigning confusion is fertile ground for new and powerful solutions. Buddha's old saw is swung into action: a crisis is also an opportunity. The previous chapters have acquainted us with the crises. Let us see if we can find the opportunities.

THE GAP

For most Americans, discussing the achievement gap that was described and quantitatively measured in chapter 9 is socially unacceptable. Its obviousness, and especially its persistence, makes us squeamish.

No public opportunity has been spared to gloss over it, cover it up, or pretend it does not exist. We are told we are all the same. Since we all bleed red, we must also have the same interests, talents, and desires, for ourselves and for posterity. Any noted differences are therefore the result of nefarious machinations that are attributed to bigotry, racism, sexism, and other social pathologies.

Paradoxically, even though the average American is pressured not to discuss the achievement gap in objective terms (which would include historical evidence and actual test and performance metrics), browbeating by academics, by the educational establishment, and by minority groups has ensured that Americans spare no expense trying to eliminate it.

Indeed, it appears that a very large portion of our educational resources are deployed for making everyone academically equal, or in other words, the goal is to make everyone above average. It sounds so simple.

As noted in many previous chapters, it is commonly alleged that educational gaps are caused not by differing abilities (nature) or interests (nature and nurture), but rather by inadequate school funding, low self-esteem, racial discrimination (personal), structural or institutional racism (systemic), the absence of compatible mentors (teachers, administrators), and poverty. Is this true?

INSUFFICIENT FUNDING

Many minority-majority public schools,[1] such as the previous examples of Highland Park, Michigan, Normandy, Missouri, Atlanta, and Georgia, receive almost twice as much state funding as schools in the rest of their home state, yet the students in these schools generally perform abysmally. The economic argument is that school performance is proportional to funding, and so, as funding increases so should academic performance. The formula is

test scores = A + B × funding

where *A* and *B* are positive constants (see also chapter 8, "Atlanta Public School Debacle"). Test results over more than a half-century, however, show that lower funding yields higher performance, so the results are more likely correlated with the following formula:

test scores = A/funding

The higher the funding, the lower the test scores, thus the lower the funding, the higher the test scores. Is it possible that reducing school funding close to zero might maximize student performance?[2]

The important factor is quality of spending. How are school financial resources used? Detroit and Newark receive massive educational budgets but only a small portion of that funding is channeled toward instruction. Either that or the portion that is channeled toward instruction goes toward the *wrong kind* and is therefore useless (see exposés by journalists David Keene, cited in chapter 8, and Dake Russakoff, cited in the above note 1).

A fair and responsible funding approach for the individual states would mandate basically equal baseline funding over the entire state since academic performance, above a certain threshold, is independent of school budget. Funding measures and policies are local matters and thus, not directly the state's concern, and if some townships or villages choose to augment state funding they can do so through voluntary millages, which amount to local property taxes.

If some neighborhoods suffer from a low property tax base, the state can compensate—*if* the state legislature approves.

If not, simpler and more direct measures akin to the Amish raising-of-the-barn are necessary. Volunteerism and community participation are needed because something never comes from nothing. In any case, the economistic argument (higher spending produces better results) should be discarded. All of the evidence presented here demonstrates the opposite.

LOW SELF-ESTEEM

Psychological research has shown that, independent of education level, black Americans have higher levels of self-esteem and self-confidence than white and Asian Americans.[3] Amy Chua has written that successful students typically feel a nagging sense of insecurity.[4] The question, "Am I good enough?" propels them toward striving and achievement. Suffice it to say that self-esteem, whether in deficit or excess, is a quantity that is not easy to measure, and therefore is likely a defective and inconclusive explanation for student underperformance.

RACIAL DISCRIMINATION (PERSONAL)

The performance level of black children is lower in all-black schools than in schools where the majority of the children are white. This statement needs no reference: it has been demonstrated by testing results since the Great Society and was also a principal impetus for forced school integration in the 1960s. Why is performance among black children lowest in all-black schools— where racial discrimination by definition cannot exist—whereas performance improves when black children submit themselves to racial discrimination as minorities in schools with whites? Why should black children endure the slings and arrows of personal racial discrimination (insults, prejudicial behavior, contempt) just to perform slightly better in school?

On July 23, 2013, *O'Reilly Factor* columnist and political commentator Charles Krauthammer said that public schools (basically all-black) at Washington, DC, are America's best-funded and worst-performing. Wasn't racial discrimination by whites in the past the cause of these problems? If so, why are D.C.'s now racially homogeneous black schools still so troubled today?

Over the years, many clever explanations have been offered to "answer" this question, but the responses do not square with the evidence of nearly half a century of experience. Sociological explanations must align with empirical evidence and the "racial discrimination" explanation does not. In fact, the evidence contradicts it.

RACIAL DISCRIMINATION (STRUCTURAL)

If America is structurally racist, why are Asian students excelling, as the extensive quantitative measurements made by Boe and Shin, Carnoy and Rothstein, and Ladner and Myslinski (see chapter 9), among many others, make clear? Shouldn't they also score near the bottom? It is not obvious why "structural racism" does not apply in their case.

Furthermore, it is not clear why, if structural racism is rampant, black Africans continue to immigrate to the United States in large—and increasing—numbers. About 10 percent of America's blacks are now real African. Why do nice black folks from Africa wish to live among white American racists with their structurally racist institutions?

I served as PhD advisor to a Nigerian student who came to the United States in 1993, earned his PhD in mechanical engineering from MSU, and stayed to work as a researcher in an American company. He later sent his daughter to MSU despite MSU's predominantly white student body and "structural/social/institutional/systemic racism." Why would he do this knowing that his daughter would be forced to underperform because of structural racism? It is clear that the structural/social/institutional/systemic racism "explanation" for black underperformance contradicts the facts and is therefore bogus. Its combustibility, coupled to its unverifiability, makes it a potent accusation.

ABSENCE OF BLACK TEACHERS/MENTORS

It has been argued that in order for a student to have academic success, he should physically resemble the teacher. To support this thesis, the researcher would have to produce two classes with exactly the same sorts of students, whose teachers use exactly the same approach, have the same personality, delivery, and expectations (standards), but who differ only in terms of their race. This test would have to be repeated thousands of times across the United States in a scientific process created by the great American physicist J. Willard Gibbs (1839–1903) called *ensemble averaging*.

The economist Walter W. Williams has produced a litany of explanations for the bogusness of the mentorship explanation.[5] Here are three quotes:

1. Attending predominantly black junior high and high schools, and graduating from the latter in 1954, I recall having no more than two, possibly three, black teachers; that was true of my primary education as well. The photograph of my 1950 junior high graduating class of 275 students, 18 of whom were white, shows no black school administrators; the principals and vice principals, and all but one of the teachers, are white. Nonetheless,

many of my classmates, who grew up in the Richard Allen housing project and with whom I've kept up over the years, managed to become middle-class adults. . . . Our role models were primarily our parents and family; any teachers who also served in that role were white, not black.[6]

2. In 2005, at my high school alma mater, Benjamin Franklin, only 4 percent of eleventh-grade students scored "proficient" and above in reading, 12 percent in writing, and 1 percent in math. Today's Philadelphia school system includes a high percentage of black teachers and black administrators, but academic achievement is a shadow of what it was yesteryear. If the dogma about role models had any substance, the opposite should be the case.[7]

3. It's not just blacks to whom the role-model dogma doesn't apply. Japanese-Americans and Chinese-Americans, as a group, score near or at the top in most tests of academic achievement. Historically, however, those children have been taught by white teachers.[8]

POOR SCHOOL FACILITIES

This topic has been extensively discussed throughout chapter 3, which demonstrated quite clearly that school facilities are not the main issue in American public K–12 education.

POVERTY

This topic has been extensively discussed in chapters 3, 4, and 5. The arguments made in those chapters do not support the thesis that poverty "explains" poor performance. Extensive research on this topic has shown that places having extreme poverty, such as parts of West Virginia, Kentucky, and Arkansas, can nevertheless produce safe neighborhoods and decent schools.

KEY IDEAS

The sociological explanations for the poor state and performance of American public K–12 schools and students have been shown to be largely without substance, unverifiable, even self-contradictory. An overwhelming part of their power lies in the incendiary rhetoric that is deployed, which makes headlines, gathers political support, stirs many hornets nests, and secures continued funding for further "studies." At every point, the application of careful thought and measured response, along with an appeal to scrupulously gathered facts and evidence (chapter 9), supports the diametrically opposite views.

Furthermore, it must be appreciated that the discussion in this chapter, although focused on racial issues, serves only to support the main thesis, that the underperforming 50 percent of American students requires serious alternatives to a pure academic education. Underperformers in education, like underperformers on the basketball court or the football field, must be directed toward pursuits that align with their actual talents and abilities.

NOTES

1. Detroit is one instance. Many other school systems receive funding far in excess of the norm whose academic performance is abysmal. The Newark public school system was recently examined in detail in Dake Russakoff, "Schooled: Cory Booker, Chris Christie and Mark Zuckerberg Had a Plan to Reform Newark's Schools. They Got an Education," *New Yorker*, May 19, 2014, http://www.new yorker.com/magazine/2014/05/19/schooled. Russakoff makes it clear that numerous parasitic organizations garnered a large proportion of the funds (upwards of 20 percent for various "consulting" organizations and companies) and that the schools themselves are a hotbed of corruption. Quite simply, the money—between tens and hundreds of millions of dollars—provided by the State of New Jersey, the taxpayer, Mark Zuckerberg, and the federal government was squandered.

2. Another possibility is to use a formula such as *test scores* $= A + B \times \text{fund-}$ *ing*, where the constant B is negative, that is, *test scores* $= A - C \times \text{funding}$, where $C = -B$ is positive. When the funding is high enough, the test scores can be made to equal zero. This happens when *funding* $= A/C$.

3. Jerald G. Bachman et al., "Adolescent Self-Esteem: Differences by Race/Ethnicity, Gender, and Age," *Self Identity* 10, no. 4 (2011): 445–73. The abstract begins: "Large-scale representative surveys of 8th-, 10th-, and 12th-grade students in the United States show high self-esteem scores for all groups. African-American students score highest, Whites score slightly higher than Hispanics, and Asian Americans score lowest. Males score slightly higher than females."

4. Amy Chua and Jed Rubenfeld, The Triple Package: How Three Unlikely Traits Explain the Rise and Fall of Cultural Groups in America (New York: Penguin Press, 2014). These traits are "superiority, insecurity, and impulse control."

5. Walter E. Williams, *Up from the Projects: An Autobiography* (Stanford, CA: Hoover Institution Press, 2010).

6. Ibid., 140.

7. Ibid., 141.

8. Ibid.

Chapter 11

Clearing Up Scientific Confusion

The science of education is not an exact science like physics, where precise mathematical calculations are supported (or contradicted) by experimental measurements. Neither is education a logical discipline like linguistics, mathematics, and philosophy, where opening statements are followed by rigorous proofs. Nevertheless, education gains when the principles and tenets of the scientific approach and logic are employed in a thoughtful and reasonable manner. The astute researcher should always acknowledge and respect that education deals with human beings—students, teachers, administrators, and staff—who respond primarily to emotions and self-interest.

In education, the data are often measurements (e.g., standardized test scores) that are made for hundreds of thousands, even millions of subjects (students). Therefore, it suits a statistical analysis and any findings, no matter how tiny the errors, imply correlation and not causation. There is no causal science of "education," although there are causal sciences of aspects of education dealing with the biology, neuroscience, physiology, and the psychology of learning. Note that these sciences, being largely empirical (there are few if any mathematical deductions in biology), are not as predictable as are the hard sciences.

Guided by logic (clear reasoning) and a practical and sensible understanding of cause and effect, the measured results should say something potentially important about how students are being educated, what they prefer to learn (if anything), and how these goals might best be met. We continue our discussion of aspects of education that bring clarity to the subject, the first topic, lead poisoning, being one that, in contradiction to the discussion of sociological explanations in chapter 10, can be quantifiably measured.

LEAD POISONING

As stated, a scientifically plausible explanation for underperformance in school is lead poisoning. Research has shown that most lead poisoning originates not from paint chips but from residual lead in the soils surrounding older houses.[1] High levels were prevalent in the materials used in their construction as well as the exterior paint. Lead is also an excellent material for joining pipe sections. For this reason, it is found in old piping systems, which were built before anyone knew that lead consumption was dangerous to humans.

Children who live in such houses are often likely to present higher in-body levels of lead, which may impair the development of mental function, and can also produce personality disorders. Recent (circa 2015) groundwater (i.e., piping) problems in Flint, Michigan, show that these concerns are valid, because old piping systems must be replaced.

Lead may plausibly explain local deficiencies in performance (if the appropriate fine-tuned measurements can be made), but it is not likely that in every climate zone and region of America, the poor performance of specific racial and ethnic subgroups is explained by this single cause. Lead poisoning is nevertheless the only explanation for underperformance with any scientific credibility.

Lead poisoning has been mentioned as having deleterious effects on IQ. Interestingly, although many individuals insist that there is "no such thing" as IQ, and that measurements of it are "meaningless," there are probably few IQ nonbelievers who would allow such measurements to be made on them or their children, demonstrating once again the disconnect between pronouncements and beliefs.

ACHIEVEMENT GAP QUANTIFIED

The achievement gap discussed by Boe and Shin, Carnoy and Rothstein, and Ladner and Myslinski in chapter 9 has not substantially changed in a century. This gap in academic achievement was first observed in the early 1900s, when the average test scores of black children ranged from about 0.775 to about 0.825 of the average test scores of white children. Accounting for minor fluctuations, this ratio has since then remained remarkably constant.

Quantitative science is steadily making inroads toward explaining this fact. In the review of a book on medical anthropology, Newton E. Morton, who is on the faculty of medicine at the University of Southampton, England, states that "genetics is advancing and anthropology isn't."[2] Morton states that the study of race and IQ has "contributed far more to society than a Marxist denial of science."

Like most scientists, Morton would doubtless argue that while we cannot assert that our entire makeup has its origins exclusively in biology, we cannot discount biology: there must be biological influence on our intelligence, our behavior, and thus, on average test scores.

The best we can do is to acknowledge that, on average, an achievement gap exists. It is an average, a statistical fact, not a prescribed and fixed universal chasm. Eliminating a statistical gap is not important; rather, what is important is for each individual to perform to his ability, academic or otherwise.

Let us clarify one final point of gap confusion. Journalists (see the introduction to chapter 1) assert that as test scores for whites and Asians continue to increase, the gap is also increasing and thus American blacks are falling ever further behind. The unspoken fact is that test scores for *all* groups have been rising.

Let us consider a fictitious example for which the average score of whites in 1990 was 10 while that of blacks was 8. The black/white ratio was 8/10 = 0.8. The gap was 10–8 = 2. Ten years later, the average score of whites was 20, of blacks 16. This ratio is 16/20, the same as in 1990, but the gap is now 20–16 = 4. The *relative* performance has stayed exactly the same (blacks score at 80 percent of whites), but in *absolute* terms, the gap has doubled—thus the attention-grabbing "falling further behind" headline. Clearly, the magnitude of the gap is not the important indicator; rather, the important indicator is the score *ratio*.

Consider what happens if that ratio actually increases (although historically it has not). Say that in 2000, instead of being 16/20 = 0.8, it had risen to 17/20 = 0.85. In this case, the gap still increased (20 − 17 = 3) from 2 to 3. Journalists would still proclaim the sky is falling ("The gap increased by 50 percent!"), whereas the opposite is true: performance relative to the top-scoring cohort had substantially increased from 80 to 85 percent. An increase from 80 to 85 percent, by the way, is not a 5-percent increase but a 6.25-percent increase.

HEREDITY

Many people both inside and outside academe assert that heredity is bogus, that it has no real meaning or relevance, that it is a "social construct." We are all human beings, we belong to one species, we all bleed red, and there is no difference between the various types of humanity that is worth discussing or evaluating. We should celebrate our humanity and rejoice in our manifest samenesses.

This is a strange and counterfactual assertion to make, however, because as the following subsection makes clear, various illnesses and diseases are passed along from parent to child. Telling a child that he has a lethal disease, a genetic defect that will kill him, cannot be considered an illusory "social construct."

Heredity Ataxia in Minnesota

The genetically inherited neurological disorder called "hereditary ataxia" (Gr., "lack of order") afflicted the German-descended Schut family of Minnesota in the early 1900s and may still afflict them today.[3] The principal character of this narrative is Henry Schut, whose father died of ataxia. He researched the disease through a "family tree documenting which individuals were affected or unaffected by the disorder."[4] Only family members with ataxia could pass it along to their children, and 50 percent of those children were affected. Henry's younger brother, John, became a medical doctor whose life goal was to find a cure for the family disorder. These two brothers found that each generation was more severely afflicted than the previous: the disease struck earlier and harder.

John and medical researchers made progress but no cure has yet been found. The article explains in depth the genetics underlying what is now called SCA1. Although John himself inherited the disorder, which took his life at age fifty-one, he developed a practical means for eliminating the disease without drug intervention.

SCA1 always presented in one's early thirties as a heritable disorder. Hence, family members with ancestors who had the disorder (which implies keeping a historical record) should wait until at least their early thirties before marrying and having children. If no preliminary symptoms appeared, all was well and the terrible gene would be expunged. If symptoms presented, they could eliminate the disease from their genetic lineage by not having children. A stern solution, indeed, but in the absence of medicinal remedies, it is guaranteed to work.

In the 1950s and 1960s, when this research was being carried out, there were none of the genetic tests that are available today. Interestingly, there are still few drugs and treatment therapies available, and no clinical-stage treatments for either the hereditary or sporadic types of ataxia. The fail-safe solution for the lethal hereditary type still belongs to John: if you have it, don't pass it along to the next generation.

Heartwarmingly, the research and dedication to eradicating this illness led John Schut to establish a National Ataxia Foundation, which now spends over $1 million annually to support medical research.

Born this way has a strong appeal to the rational mindset. Various genetic traits appear to be heritable, and research is increasingly showing that though the nature/nurture debate is complicated, a level of clarity is emerging as the brambles of confusion are hacked away. Nurture is important from birth to teens, but in the later teens and twenties, as the brain matures, nature reasserts itself: when the child becomes the man, his core is revealed. You become that which you are.

There is an established, venerable poetry of our finite, imperfect human condition; also developing is a moderately accurate science. If there are physical traits, proclivities, and disorders such as the Schut family's hereditary ataxia that are genetic (heritable), do mental activities that are heritable not also exist? Is it remotely possible that the human brain is immune to genetics and heredity?

BORN THIS WAY

A massive quantity of research using aptitude tests, psychological measures of personality, and studies of genetics, all of which are in their infancy as quantitative sciences, suggests that, as for the Schut family, distinct traits appear among groups of humans, especially when they are separated geographically from other groups for long periods of time. These groups share traits that support the born this way hypothesis.

The simplest case for born this way is the Ockham's Razor argument. Various groups evolved separately having lived for tens of millennia in geographic isolation. Another, less prevalent, argument is the appearance of a spontaneous genetic abnormality or mutation that carries with it a spectrum of definite and quantifiable characteristics.

Many traits appear in these groups, some good (high intelligence, great physical strength, long life spans, etc.) and some not so good (low intelligence, various afflictions and birth defects, etc.). The available research shows that no single group of people has a monopoly on desirable traits.

A Tiger Dad I know personally relentlessly pushed his children toward intellectual pursuits and music. Why, I asked? "Because as Chinese, our children do not have the physical gifts to athletically compete. Why would I push my children into sports, where they will always lose?" This Tiger Dad has a named professorship in one of America's best Ivy League universities. His children finished advanced degrees at Ivy League and other prestigious universities. They did not compete in athletics but were excellent in the classroom and the music hall.

Do we reduce all human achievement to genetics, heritability, and biological determinism? Do we envision a world in which the attending obstetrician pronounces, upon the birth of her child, "Proud parents, here is your sprinter!" Of course not, and no competent scientist ever would speak like this. In human achievement culture counts, as do work ethic, determination, and other social factors including good fortune. In many spheres, however, the genetic code trumps the others. It is the gorilla in the living room.

Some quotes to consider are as follows:

1. Marc Breedlove: "One interesting aspect we hadn't counted on were parents of homosexuals showing up who were curious how their children became gay. But it's like Lady Gaga said: *They were born that way*" (emphasis added).[5] Breedlove, the Rosenberg Professor of Neuroscience at MSU and co-author of three college-level textbooks and more than 120 scientific articles, says, invoking the authority of scientific data, that "prenatal hormones do influence human sexual orientation." "Born this way" acquires neuroscientific cachet.
2. Continuing on the subject of homosexuality, in a 2013 *Slate* article Mark Joseph Stern alleges that research will likely never discover the "gay gene" and that the biological explanation favors a genetic defect explanation arising from a virus carried by the mother of the gay child. The genetic defect explanation implies gayness is a disorder. "Not so fast," says Stern: "There's nothing wrong with being gay: You know it; I know it; the Supreme Court knows it." One is not compelled to call the predisposition for gayness a defect, even though traits that are statistical outliers are by definition abnormal.[6]
3. Jerome Goldstein: "'Sexual orientation is not a matter of choice, it is primarily neurobiological at birth.' So said the director of the San Francisco Clinical Research Center, addressing 3,000 of the world's neurologists from around the world at the 21st meeting of the European Neurological Society (ENS) in Lisbon [in 2011]."[7]

This small sample of quotations expresses the growing consensus among scientists, medical researchers, and individuals who are comfortable with facts and logic that many traits are inherited at conception. The preceding sample addressed only homosexuality. Some traits can be suppressed or altered by the human will, but they appear to be present in our physical, genetic makeup. Other inherited traits, like hereditary ataxia, cannot be suppressed or altered by the human will but instead play out like a programmed algorithm. As with everything else in the human sciences, there are degrees.

THE GOD GENE AND DATA CLUSTERS

The individual who espouses nurture over nature asserts correctly that no single gene has been found that quantifies the difference between any two people or between the statistical mean values for any two distinct groups of people. Does that mean there is no difference?

Many claim to believe this is true, even as the credibility of this belief dissolves under what Steven Pinker calls the tide of reality. The mounting evidence implies that humans are not born equal and are also not sufficiently malleable to ever be made equal. Not only are individuals different, but the groups to which they belong also display distinct average differences.

At this date, there is insufficient scientific evidence to refute the behaviorist viewpoint, hence behaviorism has not merely survived but thrives.

Before proceeding further, let us note that the assertion that we cannot find the single gene that is responsible for the difference between any two people is a straw man. Nobody will ever find a single gene to explain complex human behavior any more than anyone will ever find the God particle of physics or a single solution for turbulence or a single cure for every type of cancer. There will always be more physics to discover. The closure problem will likely never be solved and turbulence will remain fundamentally inscrutable. Although specific types of cancer may be treatable, it will always be a destructive and terrible illness that will likely never "be cured."

Nevertheless, we do not throw up our hands. Regarding human biology, we have located collections of dominant characteristics that accurately but not perfectly enable us and our group to be biologically and scientifically classified. This is why it is possible to find in a ditch in the woods an assortment of bones, no skin remaining, and determine using forensic techniques to nearly 100 percent accuracy that said human was, for example, a 5′8″ Caucasian woman in her early thirties who died (or was murdered) *x* months ago.

This conclusion is drawn from the accumulated evidence of size and shape of skull, jaw, teeth, eye sockets, brows, muscle attachments, as well as postcranial traits such as the "dimensions, shape and orientation of various bones, joints and pelvis."[8] The race and sex of the skin and bones can today be measured extremely accurately and, as noted, even the cause of death often accurately determined.

Since there is no single God gene, how is such an accurate diagnosis forensically possible? It is possible because, as the suite or cluster of reliably measured traits or features increases, the probability of a correct diagnosis approaches to 100 percent. Cluster analysis is a well-known and highly respected technique that becomes more reliable and accurate as traits are added to the cluster. It is also one of the most powerful ways to form a scientific conclusion. In laboratories and forensic units across the world, one can test an individual's ancestry and determine race, ecotype, and biogeographical group to a certainty of about one part in a million, or 99.9999 percent accuracy.

Cluster analysis is also the technique used by a detective to solve a crime. What our trained detective requires, contra the great Sherlock Holmes, is not one grand clue but rather an accumulation of evidence, an assortment of reliable hard facts that renders the detective's conclusion nearly 100 percent certain. In legal terms, this level of certainty is defined as *beyond a reasonable doubt.*

What does cluster analysis tell us about the difference between human groups? That they exist, that they are important, and that they should be respected. As will be discussed briefly in chapter 12, these clusters appear to extend beyond physical (outwardly apparent) traits discussed here to psychological and behavioral traits that support the thesis that not everyone is an identical learner, suited to the same type and degree of education. And since we differ, a one-size-fits-all education, just as one-size-fits-all clothing, will not suffice.

NATURE THEN NURTURE

Given that differences exist (the consensus on this is—or should be—universal), what is to be done? Can defects be ameliorated? Can a lack of ability be compensated by effort? Is it the size of the dog in the fight, or the size of the fight in the dog? What is more important: nature or nurture?

Unfortunately, the standard nature versus nurture narrative implies opposition. Why must there be opposition? Saying "nature and nurture" is an improvement, but the contention in this book is that "nature *then* nurture" best mirrors reality. The last construction encapsulates what clear thinkers have always known and it agrees with the rapidly accumulating scientific evidence.

Not everyone is enamored of this construction, hence we return to one of education's central queries: Is it nature or nurture that leads to success? It is my contention here that positive attributes for learning appear early in a child's life and that it is possible to determine who will be an academic learner and who will not. A part of this is simply natural—the student is intelligent (the nature part)—and a part of it is acquired (the nurture part). And the latter can likely be influenced by family and social circumstances much more than the former.

As always, there are gray areas and "late bloomers." But focusing on these special cases merely distorts the central thesis: about 50 percent of America's youth are above-average learners and about 50 percent are below-average learners and therefore an academic education does not serve everyone.

For this reason, a young person should be exposed to, whether in the home, the neighborhood, or the school, to a wide range of activities and pursuits, which might or might not suit his talents and abilities. If that does not happen, that young person may be defined as being *ill-served* in the home, in the neighborhood, or in the school. Sometimes, though well nurtured and wisely instructed, children may forget their lessons and take the path they seem destined to follow, even when they have been very well served. Thus, nurture had its say, but nature wins the day.

As a final example of the power of nature, consider twins separated at birth (e.g., by adoption) who often have nearly identical interests, propensities, and talents. These interests, propensities, and talents range from tastes in clothing, color, and music to the types of spouses they marry to the careers they choose, to the sports teams they cheer, to the physical activities they pursue (down to the particular sports, such as cycling or snooker), and numerous other quirky, impossible-to-socially-program details. The coincidence cannot be accidental, for these separated twins were preloaded with identical DNA. The outcomes are also nearly identical, independent of nurture, as discussed in a layman's account[9] and a second, slightly more scientific account.[10]

KEY IDEAS

Much is happening in the world of science. Little of it succumbs to a political or social-interest agenda. "The gap" in academic achievement, a volatile issue, is often subjected to discussions steeped in inaccuracy, misrepresentation, and grandstanding. The proper use of ratios when discussing the gap clears away obfuscation and willful distortion of results, especially when they should be applauded, not denigrated. Heredity plays an important, perhaps central role in a person's biological life: we are often "born this way," and there is little that can be done about it. We must live with our positive and negative attributes.

The reality of biology and human physicality is clarified in the way we break down data ("data clusters") in forensics and in other pursuits (the data-driven sciences). As the data accumulates, the conclusions approach toward certainty ("beyond reasonable doubt"). Nature *then* nurture characterizes the condition and evolution of our lives. The role of nurture, while flattering to some, may often be exaggerated.

NOTES

1. Howard W. Mielke, "Lead in the Inner Cities: Policies to Reduce Children's Exposure to Lead May Be Overlooking a Major Source of Lead in the Environment," *American Scientist* 87, no. 1 (January–February 1999): 62–73, https://www.macalester.edu/~kuwata/classes/2011-12/Chem%20222/Mielke%20American%20Scientist.pdf.

2. Newton E. Morton, "Revisiting Race in a Genomic Age," review of *Revisiting Race in a Genomic Age*, ed. Barbara A. Koening, Sandra Soo-Jin Lee, and Sarah

S. Richardson, *American Journal of Human Genetics* 84, no. 4 (April 10, 2009): 429–30.

3. Nissa Mollema and Harry Ott, "One Family's Search to Explain a Fatal Neurological Disorder," *American Scientist* 101, no. 6 (November–December, 2013): 442–49, http://www.americanscientist.org/issues/pub/one-familys-search-to-explain-a-fatal-neurological-disorder.

4. Ibid., 444.

5. "We're Angels Made out of Dirt," Whom You Love, *City Pulse*, December 5–11, 2012, 12, http://lansingcitypulse.com/article-8189-whom-you-love.html. *City Pulse* is a Lansing, Michigan, alternative lifestyle newspaper.

6. Mark Joseph Stern, "Born This Way?" *Slate*, June 28, 2013, http://www.slate.com/articles/health_and_science/science/2013/06/biological_basis_for_homosexuality_the_fraternal_birth_order_explanation.html.

7. Jeremy Laurance, "Gay: Born This Way?" *Independent*, June 14, 2011, http://www.independent.co.uk/life-style/health-and-families/features/gay-born-this-way-2297039.html.

8. Linda S. Gottfredson, "Resolute Ignorance on Race and Rushton," *Personality and Individual Differences* 55, no. 3 (2013): 218–23, http://www1.udel.edu/educ/gottfredson/reprints/2012RaceandRushton.pdf.

9. Peter Miller, photographs by Martin Schoeller, "A Thing or Two about Twins," *National Geographic*, January 2012, http://www.nationalgeographic.com/magazine/2012/01/identical-twins-science-dna-portraits/.

10. Ker Than, "A Brief History of Twin Studies," *Smithsonian.com*, March 4, 2016, http://www.smithsonianmag.com/science-nature/brief-history-twin-studies-180958281/.

Chapter 12

Groups, Gaps, and Testing

Before proceeding on the controversial topic of groups, gaps, and testing, I must make an important qualifier, quoting from a lengthy article by the libertarian political scientist Charles A. Murray: "The concepts of 'inferiority' and 'superiority' are inappropriate to group comparisons."[1] Anyone who extrapolates from discussions of group differences to eugenics and then concentration camps is being terribly disingenuous.

That qualifier being made, this chapter addresses the core issue of this book: that *a very large percentage* of American public school students do not gain by and have no business being academically educated through the twelfth grade. What they *would* benefit most from is a healthy supplement of vocational education and training in practical skills, while never forsaking a continued and crucial emphasis on our shared American culture and history.

In this chapter, I attempt to clear up some of the confusion about groups, group categorization, and how all of this is handled. For many people, this is an odious matter, but the scientific method plus thousands of years of observation—and in some cases experiment—has led us to the inexorable truth that we are different from one another. The groups of people discussed in this book are academic performers and academic nonperformers regardless of race, ethnicity, religion, or any other category into which they may be placed.

GROUPS EXIST

Groups are a basic feature of social, political, and economic organization. We structure our daily lives around groups and group structures (family, friends, associates and acquaintances, etc.); however, many people today reject the concept of the group and of group differences by pretending to adhere rigorously to the Enlightenment concept of the individual. Such people often say they belong to a group called *human beings*. In saying so, they must also reject the evidence, which amply demonstrates that isolated populations evolve unique traits.[2]

AVERSION TO GROUPS

History teaches that the consequences of clustering individuals into groups can be dire. Soviet and other Communists demonized the peasants and the bourgeoisie (upper-middle class) and liquidated an estimated hundred million people during the twentieth century.[3] Initially, it was easy to exploit group differences to sow discord and later agitate for collective mass murder. Exhibit A: Lenin, Stalin, Mao, Pol Pot, Che, Castro, Kim—a parade of sociopaths who rained death and ruin on their own and their neighbors' peoples.[4]

In the late 1940s, John Steinbeck addressed the baleful influences of the avant-garde Soviet vision:

> I believe one thing powerfully—that the only creative thing our species has is the individual, lonely mind. . . . The group ungoverned by individual thinking is a horrible destructive principle. The great change in the last 2,000 years was the Christian idea that the individual soul was very precious. Unless we can preserve and foster the principle of the preciousness of the individual mind, the world of man will either disintegrate into a screaming chaos or go into a gray slavery.[5]

The key for Steinbeck is retaining the dignity and intrinsic value of individual thinking and being.

In addition to the negative perception of groups caused by a history of genocide, Westerners in general, whether English, German, Italian, Norwegian, Swedish, and so forth, have since the Enlightenment developed a social axiom: tribal behavior is primitive and therefore bad. The concept of Group recalls Tribe, which implies a progression: Group (= Tribe) → Primitive → Undesirable. For this reason, the word "tribal" provokes strong negative emotions in the post-Enlightenment Western mind. Categorizing individuals according to group norms with separate behavioral and other traits is contrary to the egalitarian American belief in the universal norms and ideals of humanity.

GROUP REALITY

Despite the negative connotations, groups of people share biological, psychological, social, and economic characteristics. Whether or not this is acknowledged, group differences appear in populations that have previously been geographically isolated. The genetic traits of humans descended from common ancestors cluster into subsets with strong similarities, the most obvious being external appearance. These traits are especially apparent in infants, who have not been socialized into patterns of behavior and thought. Since their physical traits and their behaviors can be spotted and categorized, and because they have no guile, psychological tests often use young children to study nascent group differences that may appear, in either amplified or disguised form, later in life.

When the number of persons of common ancestry (i.e., the tribe) is large, human social, psychological, intellectual, and other characteristics, in addition to the physical, exhibit patterns that can be discerned, categorized, and studied.

Among adults, it has been firmly established that various physiological defects appear in distinct groups. These include multiple sclerosis in North European–descended women, sickle cell anemia in West African–descended blacks, and hereditary ataxia in the Schut family of Minnesota.

As discussed in these pages, groups are not necessarily racially or ethnically or biologically based. Groups form and exist due to other characteristics as well, and for the twenty-first-century American, it probably is more socially acceptable to discuss abstract groups formed by those of like interests, capabilities, and inclinations. These might be called associations.

EXAMPLE: GROUP ACTIVITY
AND THE AIRPLANE WING

Group activity has been ascribed to the discovery and invention of the airplane wing. The discovery of the aerofoil, spelled *airfoil* in the United States, was not an obvious matter ("Why don't you just look at a bird?"). It required the concerted effort of the best scientists of the late 1800s and early 1900s. Two dominant groups, English and German scientists/engineers, played the major role.

In discussing the contributions of F.W. Lanchester, David Bloor, author of a history of the aerofoil, states that the German assessment of Lanchester's work "rested on the appeal to shared standards, common to a group of otherwise diverse individuals" whose "outstanding characteristic was its *systematic and shared nature*. The German understanding of Englishman Lanchester's work, in other words, had the character of a concerted action by a group."[6] He adds that "the technical arguments . . . suggest that the response to [Lanchester's] work was not a disruption on the rational working of science but a routine example of it."

In other words, the group of German scientists participated "in a shared scientific culture" in which distinct patterns of thought and habits of work prevailed. It was ultimately the German philosophy and approach—not the English school—that led them to develop the modern airfoil.

Thus, group activity takes many forms ranging from the loftiest (scientific) to the lowliest (criminal). Their central feature is the shared understanding, with cultural, civilizational, historical, and genetic roots that cannot be ignored, discounted, or excised from any discussion of the same. There is nothing universal about a particular group's vision or even its development among a larger group of individuals; it may also be nested, a group within a group.

In the case of the airfoil, there were German and English scientists who had clearly evolved (how, exactly?) different views on the approaches used in their discipline. These views did not occur in a vacuum but in a culture, a milieu, a setting shaped by a shared history, by the ambient civilization and all its attributes (language, etc.), and also, quite likely, by the genetic inheritance of these persons, which influenced the way they thought about things, including science and the airfoil.

GROUP BEHAVIOR

Biological science, the genome project, and mathematical biology addresses issues of group behavior. Humans and all animals possess DNA sequences that make possible the appearance of physical and mental traits. The huge variety of human behavior makes the exact influence of genetics on behavior impossible to decipher. Nevertheless, one cannot despair, because large data sets may gainfully be studied not as theoretical science but rather by fitting them into a conceptual framework. This may be the best one can do with an unwieldy, complex problem.

Distinct traits that appear in large numbers produce statistically quantifiable information on human biology and also on human behavior. The sum effect of these individual behavioral attributes is characterized by the statistics for carefully defined groups. This has begun for biological (physiological) diseases such as hereditary ataxia (chapter 11). Behavioral traits between groups, being psychological and social in addition to physiological, can be compared only when there are reasonable matches between environments, leaving internal differences as the only explanation. Thus, it is feasible to compare measured differences in school performance in two communities with identical income levels, populations, and quality of facilities.

Additional comparisons are made by successively tightening the constraints. In addition to the earlier mentioned matches, the religious composition of the two regions being studied can be rendered identical. In this way, the variables—(1) facilities, (2) income, (3) population level, and (4) religion—are eliminated from consideration (or, controlled for), leaving educational performance as the free variable.

LEWONTIN'S FALLACY

A careful analysis will disaggregate the statistics and thereby attempt to delineate cause from effect and magnitude of effect. This was discussed in the analyses of chapter 9. Variances are respected because critics of group averages often assert that the differences within any group are larger than those across groups. This may be true: the peaks of the average values may be close enough that the first variances overlap. Individual members of one group often closely resemble members of another group, even though average group differences exist. Nevertheless, the peaks of the average distributions differ as do the variances, and thus the curves are separate and distinct.

A common source of confusion, Lewontin's Fallacy, arises because the critic customarily isolates only one specific trait. In discussions of the human races, the common culprit is skin color and the usual comment is: "What does skin color have to do with X, Y, or Z?" This critic is, in an important respect, entirely correct. Isolating one trait, that is, skin color, cannot possibly characterize major quantitative differences between groups, even though skin color is a crucial evolutionary adaptive trait.[7]

The problem with choosing only one trait in the discussion of difference can be illustrated by an example based on the discussion of cluster analysis presented in chapter 11. Basketball, baseball, football, and soccer each use a ball and so, according to Lewontin, they must be indistinguishable sports. Ball, like skin color, is not sufficient as a determinant trait. In order to distinguish between various ball sports, we require more data. Let us specify the number of players. If five players, we have basketball. If nine players, we have baseball. If eleven players, soccer. And if twenty-two, football. Two traits are needed to determine the ball sport.

If, instead of specifying the number of players (since, at any given time, football also fields eleven players), we specify the type of playing surface, its size, and the type of athlete who plays on it (tall and quick = basketball; strong and muscular = football; quick reflexes and exceptional visual acuity = baseball; high endurance and running stamina = soccer), we might require more data, since "strong and muscular" also describes a wrestler, for example. But then, wrestling is not a ball sport.

As we continue to add traits, we should quickly learn exactly what sport we are describing. The quickest and easiest approach, of course, would be the shape and appearance of ball. What is required in order to make meaningful comparisons is a well-chosen collection of traits, only one of which is "ball." This is exactly what those who fall victim to Lewontin's Fallacy fail—or refuse—to do. In order to know something we must accumulate clusters of facts, not isolated facts.

GROUP LEARNING AND REINFORCEMENT

Group development and improvement is self-reinforcing. If all pairs of oppo-site sex individuals in a community (tribe, clan) make wise choices of mate and raise their children well, these children will (1) possess the genetic mate-rial of intelligent, thoughtful parents; (2) benefit by associating with others in their tribe, or clan, who support those traits. The community that reinforces individual talent with group virtue essentially pulls itself up by its bootstraps: nuclear family success is compounded by collectively reinforced gain. In this *cycle of virtue*, the rich get richer (see chapter 1, "Teachers and Student Outcomes") and everyone gains.

A SCIENCE DIGRESSION

There is an analogy of human group behavior with the distinctive, measurable behavior of matter. A cubic centimeter of 10^{19} oxygen molecules (O_2) at one atmosphere pressure and room temperature behaves differently than a cubic centimeter of argon (Ar); the former can induce metals such as iron to rust, whereas the latter cannot. Similarly, copper (Cu), a solid at room tempera-ture, conducts electricity, whereas polymethylmethacrylate (Plexiglas, or PMMA), also solid at room temperature, does not.

It is not possible to ascribe collective behavior to a few molecules. Ten molecules of copper placed side-by-side do not have a measurable conduc-tivity or an elastic modulus. Only when large numbers (thousands, millions) of these molecules bond to form a coherent solid material or continuum (a tribe) will they demonstrate characteristic physical traits and properties. The density, specific heat, electrical conductivity, thermal conductivity, electric permeability, heat of fusion, and heat of liquefaction are material properties that the pure substance (O_2, Ar, Cu) possesses in the aggregate, as a group.

The science of vast numbers of molecules is an advanced, precise science called *continuum mechanics*. It is one of the most mathematically developed and accurate of all disciplines of physics.[8] We call these atomic behaviors by the name *physical properties*, which have been measured and are listed in scientific and engineering books and tables.

In addition, collections of identical atoms possess traits that could not nec-essarily be expected from the individual molecules. A solid of a certain type may crack, whereas another will deform. These collective (group) properties are described as *brittleness* and *ductility*, respectively.

It is almost impossible to predict these behaviors from the study of indi-vidual atoms, although limited headway is being made in computational chemistry. Not until they form bonds in the aggregate do these behaviors become manifest. Nevertheless, it is the structure of the individual atoms that permits the various types of bonds to form. From that bonding arises collective, predictable continuum behavior.

As always, the boundaries of science keep being pushed outward, and there is much active research on extending molecular models across this continuum/molecular overlap region. Currently, it is called *nanoscience* and its home is mostly in chemistry, and also in physics and materials science/ engineering. It is a dynamic and exciting field of research.

Many materials possess similar properties but they have different values (magnitudes). Diamond is harder than copper, which is a ductile substance (hence we can extrude it). Occasionally, groups of materials will have a subset of material properties with nearly identical values. However, they may differ completely in their other material properties. One material may be clear, another opaque, even though the brittleness of both is identical. The differences in values imply that the materials differ from one another. One would not use water to lubricate a piston, or wood for an engine block, or copper for windows because these materials do not possess the required desirable properties.

In the collection-of-molecules analogy, we know humans are not molecules. However, a group of humans possesses average composite physical traits such as characteristic ranges of height, hair color, leg length, torso length, lung capacity, liver size, heart-pumping ability, and cranial capacity, which we may refer to as human physical properties that characterize specific physical attributes. These human physical properties are analogous to saying that a material has a mass, a density, or a specific heat.

Moving from the obvious to the sublime, we know that materials possess constitutive properties. One of these is diffusivity, whose magnitude describes how readily molecules move by diffusion from one place to another. These constitutive properties are what we call *derived quantities*: they arise not as primitive definitions, as do mass or density, but as the consequence of a theory that has been developed in order to describe the material behavior. For example, the diffusivity coefficient arises from a theory of diffusion in matter. The simplest theory of diffusion of matter is the theory of Fickian Diffusion. The scientist then treats the material as obeying Fickian diffusion and measures the Fickian diffusion coefficient that corresponds to this specific mathematical theory. In this way, a whole slew of constitutive attributes, such as diffusion coefficient (Fickian Diffusion), viscous coefficient (Newton's Law of Viscosity), and conduction coefficient (Fourier's Law of Conduction), are specified for our material.

In a similar manner, important human traits can only be determined indirectly, since there is no objective method to determine a person's bravery, faith, seductiveness, sense of humor, or wisdom. These inferred attributes are measured, if at all, by indirect means unrelated to thermometers, weigh scales, and yardsticks. Furthermore, the list of constitutive traits includes impulse control, personality, social behavior, and many others, which have been deemed important for specific aspects of human development. Having a "good personality" is always helpful for success in the real world. But how, exactly, does one measure a good personality?

STANDARDIZED TESTING

Psychologists have made a huge effort to define and then measure human constitutive attributes. One of these attributes, impulse control, is measured by the "marshmallow test," the goal of which is to quantify one's ability for the deferral of immediate gratification. In this test, a child is placed in a room in front of a table upon which sits a delectable morsel, the marshmallow (or candy bar, or some other sugar-laden treat). The child is permitted to eat the treat when the examiner leaves the room. If the child waits until the examiner returns, he will receive a second treat.

Childhood deferral of gratification correlated surprisingly well with adult life accomplishment in education, employment, social standing, and financial prosperity. In fact, the deferral of gratification test produces a better correlation with life success than IQ. Why is that? Because the marshmallow test is not only a pure intelligence test but also accounts for important factors such as future-awareness, greed, indulgence, patience, and reward-concept. These qualities are apparently beneficial (future awareness, patience) or destructive (greed, indulgence) for attaining what we call life success.

Pencil-and-paper intelligence tests measure two things. One is a person's capacity for abstract thought or fluid intelligence, consisting of mathematical relationships in which a person uses his mental agility to solve abstract logico-mathematical brain teasers. The second thing intelligence tests measure is knowledge or crystallized intelligence, consisting of what we learn from experience, by cramming, or having helicopter parents.

These tests include abstract thinking to varying degrees: LSAT, MCAT, GRE, military tests of intelligence, Wonderlic (a NFL test given to incoming draft picks), ACT, SAT, IQ, New York Regents Exams, police exams, firefighter exams, engineering EIT exams, state bar (law) exams, top software company tests (Google, Microsoft, Apple), and international tests (PISA). Some tests are dominantly fluid (or abstract, or g-loaded), whereas others, like the firefighter or police tests, are crystallized (experience-based, or practical).

Abstract intelligence tests measure reasoning ability, which may be referred to as one's mental horsepower. How many bulbs can this brain light up? These tests also measure intelligence that is valuable in a knowledge-based technological society, which happens to be the society in which we live.

Abstract intelligence tests produce a consistent pattern. Caucasians *as a group* on average score higher than blacks, American Indians, and other minority groups. These differences are not unique to America, or even to North America, but appear to fit a worldwide pattern.[9] Two genetic groups that generally score higher than Caucasians are Ashkenazi-descended Jews and Northeast Asians such as Japanese, Northeastern Chinese, and Koreans.[10] The scores of Ashkenazi-descended Jews, on average, are one standard deviation above the average white/Caucasian/Gentile score. In standardized testing, this is an important difference.

These results have been categorized and analyzed in so many places that it is unnecessary to do more than briefly summarize them here.[11] To my knowledge, the most recent measurements have never contradicted the previous measurements. I am not an expert on IQ research but have spoken with many individuals who are and who say without exception that academic and professional psychologists accept research results on IQ and IQ differences. It is largely because of America's legacy of slavery that they become squeamish about the persistent gaps in the results. Although the absolute numbers may differ, and the gap between one set of tests and another may change slightly, the order of the predictions and the percent differences between the results are practically identical.

This offends egalitarians and activists ("social justice warriors") who extrapolate from IQ differences to undesired social policies and outcomes. An industry has arisen to suppress information and to mine for exotic rationalizations for the disparities. As a consequence, stating IQ differences openly and discussing them publicly can be a career-ender in the current social climate.

As one example of an article in which the reasoned, scholarly discussion of IQ, SAT, and other standardized tests results produced hundreds of vitriolic denunciations, see the comments section to "Yes, IQ Really Matters: Critics of the SAT and Other Standardized Testing Are Disregarding the Data," by David Z. Hambrick and Christopher Chabris, published in *Slate* in 2014.[12] Amazingly, the question of whether IQ should even be measured was subjected to opposing "Yes" and "No" viewpoints a few years earlier in the science journal *Nature*.[13]

Let us recall the various athletic assessments made at the NFL combine, a spate of tests that measures running speed, strength, endurance, agility, and jumping ability. Everyone knows that high NFL combine scores do not guarantee professional success, which also depends on attitude and work ethic (mental traits), resistance to pain (not measured in the Wonderlic), and avoiding injury. The last is often simply luck. The Wonderlic's measurements, therefore, are indicative of the *potential* to be a top-caliber NFL athlete.

In a similar manner, intelligence tests constitute a measure, albeit imperfect, of the mental horsepower of a person. Whether (or how) one employs one's mental horsepower is the subject of deeper, more abstract tests of the kind developed by psychologists, like the marshmallow test. Intelligence tests, therefore, are a measure of one's *potential* for abstract thought.

STANDARDIZED TESTING—NOT THE BE-ALL
AND END-ALL

Standardized testing is not perfect, but, when done well, it is the best we have. The pushback against this type of testing, along with the associated group identification, is massive. Assuming the measurements are correct and the statistics are honestly gathered (i.e., there is no conspiracy to suppress information), we are discussing raw facts. The questions is how does one deal with facts?

It appears there are four ways to deal with these facts:

1. Deny and suppress them, by protesting that testing is biased and discriminatory and designed to produce a specific, nefarious outcome. Underperformance of various groups is explained by characterizing tests using inflammatory language. This is currently the most common tactic.
2. Admit that differences exist but then assert that the tests really do not measure anything important other than pencil-and-paper skills, even though we live in a pencil-and-paper world. This is currently the second most common tactic.
3. Admit that differences exist and attempt to direct students toward programs of academic education that align with their abilities. This was the original justification in the early 1900s for such tests, and is, of course, the most reasonable and humane approach, for it allows diamonds in the rough to be discovered based on ability, not financial/social/familial connections.[14] It is currently the next-to-least common tactic.
4. Acknowledge that differences exist and attempt to direct students not only toward programs of academic education that align with their academic abilities but also toward programs of development (apprenticeships, internships, training) for individuals who display a demonstrable absence of abstract academic thinking ability. This, the hardest sell of all, is the tactic I advocate in this book.

STANDARDIZED TESTING—A DEFENSE

The reasons most people oppose standardized testing often have more to do with emotion, and correspondingly, less to do with objective analysis.

Although academic and professional psychologists and social scientists universally support intelligence testing, "intelligence reporting" is the forbidden term of social science. Thus, many individuals who are not social scientists but are influenced by the tenets of current social science emit many inanities, including that IQ is simply a measure of what the testing establishment and the social system regards as important ("what IQ tests test for"), or that its purpose is to "classify people secretly," or that the tests are culturally biased.[15]

No one has ever claimed that intelligence testing is perfect or that it characterizes everything we needed to know about people. Also, it is not clear why it would be claimed that the testing establishment and the social system, that is, those who devise and administer IQ tests, are aligned against the general public good.

Thus, the American public has been conditioned to distrust intelligence testing. Even more loathsome is what we have been led to believe the tests imply. Intelligence research seems to run against our primal impulse to feel good about ourselves. Americans believe that, for every person, the sky is the limit.

Despite the ill-will that often surrounds it, however, intelligence tests are universally used. Police and fire departments screen their applicants. In 2012, to own a pistol legally in Michigan, one had to pass a written test: if one could not read and also pass the test, one could not own a handgun.[16] To be drafted into the NFL, one must perform reasonably well on the Wonderlic: a good player needs to remember the playbook and think fast. To serve in the U.S. military, one must pass an intelligence test. To gain admission to college, students take the SAT and ACT; to be accepted into law school, one must score reasonably well on the LSAT; and to practice as a lawyer, one needs to pass the bar exam. To practice medicine, a doctor must take the MCAT and pass various state medical licensing board exams. Those who apply to graduate school must take the GRE, and for various subspecialties, there is a GRE for physics, mathematics, and engineering.

Crossword puzzles, Sudoku puzzles, chess strategies and endings, and various *American Scientist* and *Scientific American*[17] monthly math puzzles are intelligence tests. *New York Times* Sunday crossword puzzle aficionados post the time it took to solve them, saying, in effect, "Look how smart I am." These challenging games and quizzes constitute, at the very least, informal, voluntary tests of intelligence that many people greatly enjoy.

Back to the point, is it possible to devise g-loaded tests that are independent of cultural details?

That is indeed one of the goals in standardized testing. Scientists have sought, ever since intelligence tests were constructed, to develop questions that reflect pure, unbiased, or raw intelligence. Such questions measure spontaneous, fluid, or unpracticed intelligence, not experience or wisdom.

The latter can be gamed. The goal of a true intelligence test is to cleanse it of cultural and social influence, in order to eliminate social bias and the implicit noxiousness of cramming. It has been known for a long time that an intelligence test that favors the grind is not a true intelligence test.

Research across many decades, and increasingly more lately, has shown that a substantial part of intelligence is heritable. The brain, like the body, developed differently in geographically separate regions. Different types and amounts of nutrition, different climate, biological and ecological constraints, behavioral choices, and patterns dictated principally by geography conspire to yield, over thousands of years and tens if not hundreds of generations, unique physical and mental talents. It is illogical to assume there is not "brain diversity" to at least as great a degree as physical diversity and it is impossible to argue in favor of the one while denying the other.

INDIVIDUALS IN GROUPS

The groups discussed here are of students whose abilities and interests—irrespective of race or gender or social standing (socioeconomic status)—place them in quantitatively different academic or nonacademic categories.

Under discussion in this book on K–12 American public education is the distinction based on ability and talent regardless of where it appears. There are no quotas on the basketball court for slow and undersized persons of whatever ethnic or racial category. There should likewise be no quotas for "underrepresented minorities" in any program of education. In order to ascend to this understanding, one must get comfortable with the fact that in any population, about half operate below the mean value. A humane and inclusive system of public education deals with that lower half of students.

GROUPS OF STUDENTS

Standardized test scores, the classroom accomplishments and behavior of students, and observations of them made by teachers, parents, neighbors, and members of the community from kindergarten to the eighth grade amply demonstrate who is well suited for excellence in academics. My thesis—one-size-does-not-fit-all—when fleshed out, shows that this number applies at most to approximately 25 percent of the student body, with the remaining educable cohort in the top 50 percent (i.e., the next 25 percent) being decently educable.

For this reason, students should be grouped according to academic ability and other ability (talent). At about the age of thirteen, students should be directed toward education programs that align with their abilities, interests, and circumstances. By that age, it should be quite clear whether the student is a learner, what he can and will learn, and what are his talents and interests. The student's environment and resources are also important components in this calculation, as the many examples discussed throughout this book have shown.

Students should be grouped by evidence of ability and talent and not by any other measure. If standards are followed (see below) there can be no quotas.

TYPES OF SCHOOLS

American K–12 public schools as reimagined can focus on (1) academics, where education focuses on book learning; (2) academically related skills, where education acquires a significant hands-on component (the various arts) sometimes referred to as "visual-spatial skills"; and (3) practical skills, where education is directed toward career and training for various kinds of employment. Requirements for specific skills change rapidly as workforce needs evolve. Hence, a practical education must also be general so that a learned skill is not obsolete after graduation.

In addition to the students who fit into these three categories, there is a segment of the population who drop out and often engage in activities that offer little tangible benefit for society. It does America no good to pretend that this segment of society does not exist, or to acknowledge it grudgingly and deal with it punitively through the legal system. These former students are generally noneducable, although the occasional exception can be found, usually with great fanfare. As mentioned, the relevant option for these students is one that existed long ago but for alleged budgetary reasons has been abandoned: reform school.

OFFICIAL PRETENSE

As stated many times in these pages, the great failure of American public education originates from the official pretense that every student possesses the various traits, good or bad, in equal measure.

The discussion in this book has attempted to address and offer some options to begin clearing up the major sources of confusion affecting the approach to and evaluation of America's K–12 schools. Our public school system, which pretends that everyone is suited for and capable of an academic education, needs an overhaul that aligns with nature that teaches us that inequality is the foundation of the human condition. Inequality is a good thing and in fact is the source of true diversity. Sending children to school with the belief that they all will become doctors, scientists, engineers, mathematicians, lawyers, and economists is a delusion.

HARD DECISIONS

The decisions we make on behalf of our young Americans may seem harsh, and final. Telling someone he does not qualify is difficult, whether it is for the cheerleading team or AP history. A student usually knows when he not performing to standard, and what the administrator believes is a painful decision is often met instead with relief. Nevertheless, a great amount of hypocrisy is involved in making such "hard" decisions, for a simple reason.

America, as we all know, is especially well versed in the "winners" and "losers" mindset. Everyone knows who the fastest runner is in class, who is (or is not) good looking, or who is musically or artistically talented. The most egregious discriminative category by far in America is sports, where sorting is done purely based on athletic talent. We know exactly who "the best" is because it is obvious, even to those with no interest in sports.

This state of affairs behooves me to close with an important question: Do we in America feel as strongly about the value of cultivating our intellectual talents and abilities as we do about our athletes? If yes, then the program of this book is relevant and appropriate.

NOTES

1. Charles Murray, "The Inequality Taboo," *Commentary*, September 1, 2005, https://www.commentarymagazine.com/articles/the-inequality-taboo/.

2. Charles Darwin, *The Origin of Species by Means of Natural Selection: 150th Anniversary Edition* (London: J. Murray, 1859; Mineola, NY: Dover Thrift Edition, 2006).

3. Stéphane Courtois et al., *The Black Book of Communism: Crimes, Terror, Repression*, ed. Mark Kramer, trans. Jonathan Murphy and Mark Kramer (Cambridge, MA: Harvard University Press, 1999). Numerical breakdowns and statistics are provided for the various communist countries. Regardless, they were remarkably efficient killers.

4. Some might argue that those people killed by Communist dictators would have died anyway. This would be correct, in a pathological way, although all of these people died in misery, often murdered by bullet to the back of the head, often much sooner than they would have died by other causes, and, if they died young enough, before they were able to put their genetic stamp upon evolution.

5. John Steinbeck, letter to John O'Hara, June 8, 1949. Cited in John Steinbeck, *Sweet Thursday*, ed. Robert Demott (1954; New York: Penguin Classics, 2008).

6. David Bloor, *The Enigma of the Aerofoil: Rival Theories in Aerodynamics, 1909–1930* (Chicago: University of Chicago Press, 2011), 196–97.

7. Daniel T. Ksepka, "The Penguin's Palette: More than Black and White," *American Scientist* 104, no. 1 (2016): 36–43, http://www.americanscientist.org/issues/feature/2016/1/the-penguins-palette-more-than-black-and-white. Ksepka discusses the crucial implications of their color on the penguin's reproduction, evolution, and survival.

8. Gerhard A. Holzapfel, *Nonlinear Solid Mechanics* (Chichester, UK: John Wiley and Sons, Ltd., 2000). This book provides a rigorous mathematical exposition of the basic structure of modern continuum mechanics. A less technical but scholarly and masterful set of essays on the subject of continuum mechanics and its relation to science and the study of history was written by natural philosopher Clifford A. Truesdell, *An Idiot's Fugitive Essays on Science: Methods, Criticism, Training, Circumstances* (New York, Berlin, Heidelberg: Springer-Verlag, 1984). Anyone interested in science should read these outstanding essays.

9. Warehouses of books have been written on the subject of IQ. Two works that address IQ and national wealth patterns are Richard Lynn and Tatu Vanhanen, *IQ and Global Inequality* (Augusta, GA: Washington Summit Publishers, 2006) and *IQ and the Wealth of Nations* (Westport, CT: Praeger, 2002). A nonscholarly version of these findings is available at "World Rankings of Countries by Their Averages," IQ Research, https://iq-research.info/en/page/average-iq-by-country. A critique is found in Thomas Volken, "IQ and the Wealth of Nations: A Critique of Richard Lynn and Tatu Vanhanen's Recent Book," *European Sociological Review* 19, no. 4 (September 2003): 411–12.

10. This requires disaggregating the statistics, by filtering out the Ashkenazi Jews from the general Caucasian population (leaving Gentile Caucasians). There may be other groups that also score higher or lower than the average, but they are not often mentioned.

11. Linda Gottfredson, "Intelligence," Instant Expert, *New Scientist*, June 29, 2011, https://www.newscientist.com/data/doc/article/dn19554/instant_expert_13_-_intelligence.pdf. This article provides a gentle introduction to the concept and use of IQ measurements. In the final section, "Are We Getting Smarter?" Gottfredson states that "the idea that cultural environments have potent and widespread effects on how smart we are does not square with what we know about the high heritability of intelligence. Environmental variation contributes relatively little to the IQ differences in a birth cohort as its members mature over the decades" (viii). She also addresses the well-known "Flynn effect," in which IQs are shown to have risen substantially in the past century of IQ testing. Working backward implies that persons living as recently as the 1700s or 1800s were quite unintelligent, making it difficult to explain the ambient sophistication of the European culture and social life. Gottfredson asks, "Could the IQ (intelligence) of adults at the end of the second world war really have been 20 points less than today? That would put them in the bottom 10 percent of intelligence

by current standards, making them legally ineligible to serve in the U.S. military on grounds of poor trainability. It defies belief" (viii). IQ testing is not physical science.

12. Hambrick and Chabris, "Yes, IQ Really Matters."

13. Steven Rose, "Darwin 2000: Should Scientists Study Race and IQ? NO: Science and Society Do Not Benefit," *Nature* 457, no. 12 (February 2009): 786–88. "Darwin 2000: Should Scientists Study Race and IQ? YES: The Scientific Truth Must Be Pursued," by Stephen Ceci and Wendy M. Williams, immediately follows in the same volume of *Nature*.

14. David Z. Hambrick, personal communication with author, 2016.

15. Comments of this kind were extracted from the thread responding to Nicholas Kristof, "It's a Smart, Smart, Smart World," op-ed, *New York Times*, December 12, 2012, http://www.nytimes.com/2012/12/13/opinion/kristof-its-a-smart-smart-smart-world.html, who discussed the apparent trend for IQ scores to rise, over time, for all groups. The piece, which generated over 300 comments, does not mention that for comparisons of identical racial groups, those who were raised in the advanced countries scored much higher than their ancestral relatives in the third world. Supporters of IQ and intelligence measurements have never denied the positive influences of good nutrition and intellectual stimulation.

16. For better or worse, by 2016, the laws changed and a written test is no longer required.

17. *Scientific American* employed a writer of popular mathematics, Martin Gardner, who in addition to writing articles on mathematical subjects, which have been described as "models of clarity and elegance for introducing fresh and engaging ideas in mathematics in non-technical ways," also formulated various games and puzzles for readers interested in confronting a mental challenge. The "Mathematical Games" column in *Scientific American* began in January 1957 when Gardner was forty-seven years old. See the guest blog post by Colm Mulcahey, "The Top 10 Martin Gardner Scientific American Articles," *Scientific American*, October 21, 2014, for a discussion of Garner and his work, https://blogs.scientificamerican.com/guest-blog/the-top-10-martin-gardner-scientific-american-articles/.

Index

About the Author

Indrek S. Wichman received his PhD in Mechanical and Aerospace Engineering (MAE) from Princeton University in 1983. He worked for two years at the NIST Building and Fire Research Laboratory on fire spread and combustion and then, starting in 1986, at Michigan State University, where he remains on the faculty of mechanical engineering as a full professor. His research is predominantly in combustion science with forays into green roof analysis, automotive engines/energy, and the study of crack formation in solids. His teaching focuses on Combustion, Thermodynamics, Fluid Mechanics and Applied Mathematics. He is a member of the National Association of Scholars (http://www.nas.org), Sigma Xi and The Combustion Institute. Of Estonian descent, he was born in New York City.

CPSIA information can be obtained
at www.ICGtesting.com
Printed in the USA
BVOW09s2323181117
500722BV00003B/9/P